Edinburgh Review 138

Edinburgh Review
Editor: Alan Gillis
Assistant editor and production: Jennie Renton
Marketing and events: Lynsey May

Advisory Board: Janice Galloway, Kathleen Jamie, Robert Alan Jamieson,
James Loxley, Brian McCabe, Randall Stevenson, Alan Warner

Published by Edinburgh Review, 22a Buccleuch Place, Edinburgh EH8 9LN
edinburghreview@ed.ac.uk
www.edinburgh-review.com

Individual subscriptions (3 issues annually) £20 within the UK; £28 abroad.
Institutional subscriptions (3 issues annually) £35 within the UK; £43
abroad. Most back issues are available at £7.99 each. You can subscribe
online at www.edinburgh-review.com or send a cheque to Edinburgh
Review, 22a Buccleuch Place, Edinburgh EH8 9LN

Edinburgh Review 138
What Light Remains

ISBN 978-0-9564983-9-7
ISSN 0267-6672

© the contributors 2013
Printed and bound in the UK
by Bell & Bain Ltd, Glasgow

Edinburgh Review
is supported by

CREATIVE SCOTLAND
ALBA | CHRUTHACHAIL

Contents

What Light Remains

Martin MacInnes

Farm

I had not seen the family in twenty-one years, since my grandfather's funeral here at the over-full cemetery just above the waterline, gravestones beaten and inscriptions weathered to illegibility. There were few trees and it was cold and bright. Mountains across on the mainland. Some of the gravestones had been maintained, enough of them for me to guess that maybe a third of all the dead here had our name. We went to the bright fields. Forty roe deer on the hill to the south, returning somewhere after the night. I heard of sea-eagles attacking stags, swooping down suddenly with massive wing-weight, aiming to stun and to kill. We left feed for the sheep and the cattle and in the late afternoon I became a sort of barely competent gatekeeper, running about the fields opening and closing the gates at relatives' instruction, as they drove the sheep on and sifted them and sorted them ahead of the sale they would go to in Dingwall the next day. Bureaucracy has it that all livestock are to be individually labelled several ways; they grabbed the horns of the rams and stapled into their ears, checking teeth as well for signs of age, brittle, jerking animal legs stabbing out in mild panic. Next to a skull and some threads of wool there was another freshly dead sheep – strange, the two having both come to die at the same spot weeks apart, with all the fields and hills to choose from. I was taught how to dig a grave – obvious techniques I hadn't even thought of – of course you first draw the shape of the animal in the ground, of course you then leave the turf to one side to be spread on finally over the compacted soil and the cut roots, which you stamp on. In the evening we ate fish and took whisky while I heard stories that were to me surprising and delightful – these men had sung! – and looked through photographs – most of them out of doors, in summer, in fields – and funeral notices, tributes to nurses and farmers, many of whom died young.

Hunting was instrumental in the brain expansion of pre-human hominid groups several million years ago. Neanderthals – whose brain was larger than homo sapiens' – had a diet almost exclusively of meat. Meat contains more protein per gram than plant, giving more excess energy to the body. And catching larger and faster prey could only be done through group cooperation, which valued, and so increased, empathy and communication. Use of fire – possibly first suggested by lightning hitting trees, whose torched branches could be removed and carried – certainly fostered a sense of community. Charred cadavers led to cooking and food storage and distribution, furthering the social contracts that defined the descendant species. Consumption of other animal bodies played a massive and labyrinthine role in the development of the brain, with symbolic capacity, social sophistication, and anatomical dimensions feeding off each other in a positive loop.

Sixty-thousand years ago the world's human population was around a quarter of a million. Three-thousand years ago it was sixty million. Today it is seven billion.[1] This growth has been enabled, not by hunting, but by agriculture, which arose independently at least eight times in a period beginning twelve thousand years ago. Agriculture yields more food than hunting does. Families could grow. Small communities developed into towns and cities.

With the end of the last ice-age an ecological period begun in which farming was possible. It was warmer and wetter and the atmosphere, containing higher levels of CO_2, was more conducive to plant growth. Farming may even have arisen through the observable fertility of human latrines, blooming seeds of fruit.

There are more people alive today than the total sum of all dead. Birthrate, under agriculture, increased by orders of magnitude. The human mass unfolded to occupy and transform the major part of Earth.

Despite the food surplus, generations of farmers suffered. The new cereal-based diet – rich in carbohydrate – contained far less protein than the earlier carnivorous diet. People became *smaller*. New diseases spread from the necessary intimacy with livestock, and infant mortality grew, leading to an ever higher rate of birth. After making the transition to agriculture populations had grown so quickly that a reversion to a pre-agricultural state, with its lower but healthier food production, was impossible.

There was another sheep, and it did several unexpected things. First, it was alive. It had been taken for dead, a protective assumption on our part. It was difficult to imagine it not being dead. A grown sheep cannot right itself from a fallen position, neither can it shield itself. The most significant of its weaknesses is curiosity. By opening its eyes it reviewed its environment, believing doing so was automatically advantageous, its sight always associated with power. It could not learn to deviate from its tendency to look. And now we were looking, and seeing the startling evidence of its living in the tremors and the twisting of its head. Now that it was alive, it might have made a sound. It opened its mouth but only mimed. We turned it over to its front with a quick firm push, but it made no attempt to stand. The whole of its eyes were gone. No parts hung in flayed strands, no translucent threads, no hint of neural connections or of the architecture of vision. Blood sprayed several inches of compact arcs as it turned its head. It seemed to be moaning, but it was incapable of making sound. We'd chased the raven but it waited close. It was the one bird, taking one eye at a time. Could the bird stab through and tear out the lids? It was unclear whether the lids were still attached – they would have been forced open by the pulsing blood and even if they hadn't been the pressing of the lids against whatever raw foundations remained would only have increased its pain. If the bird was unable to scythe out the lids – which seems the case – then it must have simply waited – close – for its prey to open each eye.

Several sheep gathered round, perhaps to have scared the bird away. They were unable to do this whether or not they had been inclined. They made what sounded like distressed noises. The raven waited, perched on a fence, folded in itself, caped. The instinct of the awake animal to open its eyes is so strong that it insists on its doing so even after – as? – one of those eyes is extracted. The defensive example is to close the other eye indefinitely. Is 'unnatural' the correct word to assign to the sheep seeing with one eye the other being taken and eaten? Because it wasn't unnatural – this is not an exceptional occurrence. The horror of the other eye opening directly to the waiting raven, the silent, neat, proficient bird spearing in with its beak, collapsing the wet order of the globe, making the world dark. The sheep hearing the compact feasting, the tearing and bursting, knowing what this sound is and what it means, knowing that it is edible material, that its sudden darkness – the total removal of the visible world – is due to edible material. And we looked.

The immune system is the liminal point of agency, the physical definition of self, the original attempt at drawing a line between one thing and another, organism and world. It is the automatic detection of 'other' and 'alien', the primitive expression of individual life. It is our defence against disease and the reason organ transplants are so often rejected by the recipient's body. It is the parochial intelligence of the body. In agricultural millennia human immune systems were reconfigured. The increased consumption of carbohydrates, and especially those carbohydrates that are broken down in digestion, interfered with control of blood sugar and caused metabolic problems such as diabetes. The increase in disease and in consumption of cow and goat milk exerted new pressures on the immune system.

As the immune system was altered by environmental conditions and genetic mutations, so too were other parts of the body. Over thousands of years, with an unprecedented number of new people being born at an ever greater rate, and in a radically new environment, change will occur. And the brain – intimately connected with the digestive and immune systems that are themselves being reconfigured – will not be exempt. And it is interesting, in this period of great weakness, vulnerability and change, that religion should develop.

The principles of faith, sacrifice, transformation and harvest are common to agriculture and the Abrahamic religions. It is reasonable to assume seasonal planting and rising of the yield influenced these religions. Any system that inspires faith is particularly virulent in times of hardship – another reason why it is logical that religious beginnings should coincide with this period. The organic cycles of agriculture make clear the fertility and vitality of dead objects, creating new life from soil. The first rising of plants personally sewn may have inspired feelings of religiosity and creativity and a sense of the sustenance of future generations.

Other times were spent bringing life in. He brought his hands inside a struggling sheep and eased the spill and slop of the lamb. I watched its legs ringing and chest convulsing, the dramatic interaction of its body and air, observed its liquid sheen, the mother pruning and cleaning it, waited for its urge to stand to manifest. Placenta, faeces and straw covered the floor of the barn. The nativity setting is interesting.

The cow removes itself at the approach of labour. Even in difficult steep fields it does this, getting away from the others. Any agitation might delay it, might interfere with the flow of its reflexes. This maternal exile begs appropriation, transference, the mythic – wandering in the desert, indescribable life. Afterwards the animals are curious, the other mothers sniff and inspect, clean, drink up the fertile mixtures of the ground.

A night labour in the field is a problem, difficult to monitor. There is quiet, coded debate in the kitchen, few words, a decision. There will be labour in the night. Somehow even the expression of the cow – its eyes – transmits specific information about the coming birth. It's away in the fields and soon it'll be dark. We lead her through the streams and rocks and mud, slopping and scooping towards the barn a mile off. The animal is inestimably more elegant on ground; we are strangers here, feet sinking. It's steadily darker and we are at a height over the very still sea and the black treeless coastlines of island and mainland. She wanders erratically, tries oblique rushes. By walking at the correct angle and at a reasonable distance you can usher the animal forwards, take her where you want her to go, breaking off exits to vaster moorland. We reach the barn by dark and wait indoors with television and fire, all the strange silences and loneliness of being sealed. The oilskins hanging and boots lined up by the house edge have traces of wool, iodine, blood, faeces. The television is a stream of light projecting the unconsciously ritualistic movements of mysterious figures. To watch them walking, driving, sleeping, eating, dancing, is exotic. We boil water and fill a pot, step from place to place, feel the hair of the carpets and rugs, hear the strain and creak of the wind against broad sea-facing windows. The lamps produce soft fogs of light, the turning of logs in the fire is pleasantly audible. A house is a place to sleep in and pretend that you are not out there. My eyelids are closing in. Everything is so soft. At mealtimes we ease ourselves away and talk trivia, though the obsessive repetition of commentaries on self-evident weather suggests some token acknowledgement of the authority of the outside. The exchange of personal trivia as well, the deep investigations of the minutiae of our surface preferences, in its bizarre and microscopic detail, is an oblique gesture at intimacy, a substitution, an encroaching awareness of the way people spend their days.

Less than a mile up the road is the labour. I am family but I am a guest,

I am only playing. But this is vital. His anxiety is obvious; the contradiction of needing to observe and of observation being a dangerous disturbance. We leave it as late as we can, around midnight, and step into the silence and wonderful darkness. I wait in the jeep. He waves me in and runs back to the barn door, giddy as a child, just so I can see, letting me see.

Is religion an imaginative way of understanding what our bodies are, how they are maintained and how they fit into the long stretches of time in which they are not present? It is evident that a body is nothing – it is not there – then it is made, it is there, and then it is destroyed. It is the same with a species: it will not be, then it will come to be, then it will be gone. It is also the same with a planet, and beyond a planet a galaxy, even a universe. It is a narrative that is impossible to comprehend. One imaginative response is to deny the narrative conventions of beginning, middle, end. The existence, out of nowhere, of an event, a something, is illogical. Matter is illogical, but it is. Matter instructs our imaginations.

A living body is an impossible narrative. It conducts itself – live, feeling tissue – through an unceasing going away and new-coming. It seems to be enabled to be at all by cancelling itself and re-emerging at all times. The main cellular action of a body is a giving away of itself, the repeated destruction of its constituents, repeated because it is countered by the immediate regrowth of everything always. During a body's time the finality of ending is not relevant, because the automatic self-ending of a body is its central creative process, the very thing that for a period allows it not to end. Ending has been harnessed as a growth engine. Ending is a means to going on.

The self-renewing and replicating action of the body is in accord with that of all matter, including world objects that we call inanimate or non-living such as rocks. Continents move over hundreds of millions of years as oceans evaporate and reform and support the emergence of changing organisms, radiating into species, whose populations fall into the ground or the seas or are extinguished by fire, settling again, as molecules spilled by sundered bodies, into coarser elements of the earth. A thing that is born is a different presentation of material that was already present and will be so after death. An organism – an animal, a human, a plant – is not a sudden invention, not a piece of inspiration. It is an old thing reformed, material of the age of earth.

All of the body is a tension delicately held in place, a form rejuvenating itself out of its own rot. We are distinctly unstable – the stuff we are is breaking and arising like surf. We cover the affects of our lives – the things we touch – with the invisible ash of our bodies, our last layer of skin. It is a striking liquidity, an intercourse with everything we might consider apart from ourselves. The body turns itself over, breeds itself from molecular residue. Our basic vitality, the gust of ourselves, the motor of our breath and thought, is the brilliant biology of life from death and so the motifs of our religions should come as no great surprise.

Our ideas of resurrection may be instructed by the regenerative activity of the cells that compose the thing that has ideas. It is natural that this supple discontinuousness, this resistance to narrative, should emerge in our mental activity just as in our physical. As Freud revealed the dominance of the unconscious and the fragility of the ego, the strangeness to ourselves of ourselves, and as attachment theory sketched the effects of intimacy, blurring the outlines of one person and another, and as the whole enterprise of neuroscience has come to see the brain as an uncentred organ, the mind as an undirected amalgamation of modules, one part literally not knowing another, it is implied that our mental solidity – the certainty of 'I' – is as illusory as our physical solidity. The bizarre narrative of biology, which may have it that in one sense we are never born and we never die while in another sense both actions occur simultaneously and always, is complemented by the suggestion from psychology that there is no self and thus nothing to experience such ultimate liminal stages as birth and death. If the self has never existed except as an illusion, if we accept that, then what does death become? What is it that may be faced? What may be destroyed?

Approaching the bridge that will take us from the island I am aware of the masses of earth and rock piled up and looming over oppressed cottages, a treeless vertical desert, and of the slow circular motion of our vehicle tracing the velodromic contours of the blasted rock. Under enclosing black mountains the quiet ribbon of road, the tiny white square cottages, the limp upturned boats and other remaining industrial effects sit fixed to the caldera. Everything petrified in time. The animals are being ended; two dozen sheep butting against each other and charging the gaps in the back of the lorry. The clatter of stamping and the dropping of faeces. They cannot know where they are going.

We pass the graveyard, headstones fallen and split to pieces. Everything is brave in the upheaval of the moving earth. I wonder who lives in each of these houses, and I crane my neck for evidence of a pale face by a window, a small figure shuffling into an uneven field with a basket of white linen, a blond child carrying flesh-warm eggs from a chicken coop. Directly facing the almost sheer black mountain, in grand comedy, are two white deck-chairs, several inches apart.

What are we turning over? The shooting of the eyeless sheep, I now heard, did not go smoothly: a slip of a finger in the rain and the release of the bullet at the wrong time, into the wrong part of its head. The shock of the removal of most of a face. The boots and skins scrubbed. Difficult to remove, from the house, the smell of what happened. In the last night, with family, I had almost gone to say something – *how is it that…? How do we…?* That with all of this, in all of this, there is somehow a celebration, a dawn persistence. But I said nothing.

1. The statistics on populations and genetics are drawn from *The 10,000 Year Explosion,* Gregory Cochran and Henry Harpending, 2009.

Michael Longley

Deathbed

I imagine my deathbed like my friends' love bed
Whose friends come into the house for breakfast
Every morning, robins, one long-legged, fleet,
The original, another lurking in a corner,
One searching under the bed for spiders,
One swooping from doorway to cheese-dish.

When I die I shall give them all their names.
There will be many robin generations
Coming into the house, and wrens and blackbirds
And long-tailed tits will learn from the robins
About the cheese-dish and saucer of water.
I'll leave the window open for my soul-birds.

Amelia's Poem

Amelia, your newborn name
Combines with the midwife's word
And, like smoke from driftwood fires,
Wafts over the lochside road
Past the wattle byre – hay bales
For ponies, Silver and Whisper –
Between drystone walls' river-
Rounded moss-clad ferny stones,
Through the fenceless gate and gorse
To the flat erratic boulder
Where otters and your mother rest,
Spraints black as your *meconium*,
Fish bones, fish scales, shitty sequins
Reflecting what light remains.

Cry

Your cry translates greylag-geese alarms
And, invisible out there in sea mist,
The prawn-fisherman's puttering outboard.

Fetlocks

I had thought of wind-chimes
To accompany your sleep,
But they are too airy, so
I imagine the fetlocks
Of a neighbour's Clydesdale,
Icicles in harsh weather
Tinkling at each earthy stride.

Birth-Bed

I waken in the bed where you were born
Weeks ago: the March light from Avernish
Kindles in leafless self-seeded saplings
Water-sparks, and rinses the scallop shells
And white horseshoe that decorate the porch.

This is my unassuming *nunc dimittis*
While I wait like Simeon to cradle you
Swaddled in light and shadow – vernix
And lanugo – even the wattle byre's
Rusty corrugated-iron roof's ablaze.

Zoë Strachan

Zugenruhe

Hier bitte, hier! Hier ist gut. Bitte…

The taxi passes the door of the apartment, by one block, then two. Merle wanted this, the city flashing by at speed, the sense of movement. For a second she imagines her voice isn't working, that the words are silent, but no, the driver has heard her and the taxi is pulling in to the kerb. The Fotograf is sitting in the back seat, his camera angled at the side of her face, her bad side, she thinks, not entirely seriously, as she scrambles in her purse for enough euros to pay the fare. His distance is admirable, she supposes; he wouldn't even say the word for stop. A word she can't remember, in German. It hasn't been part of her vocabulary here, hers and the Musician's.

She clambers out and walks back towards the graffiti-covered doorway, becoming aware of music in the warm air, the Fotograf's camera whirring as it adjusts to the dark of the street. She casts a glance back; he's a shadow, training the lens at the clipclop heels of her shoes. Her feet are tired, another reason for the taxi home rather than two changes on the U-Bahn. She imagines splaying her toes against cool sheets, the draught from an open window. Maybe the Musician is out on a spree and won't come home until morning. It is morning though. Until lunchtime then, that would do.

Fumbling for her key, she becomes nervous suddenly of this dark street and the shadowy little park across the road. It's as if the Fotograf isn't there at all. If someone attacked her would he intervene, or let the camera roll? He's an artist too, isn't he, like the Musician. Let it roll then. A page with tear-off strips is pasted to the door jamb, inviting her to make drinking money by selling her old CDs, or at least she thinks that's what it says. This building at least is unreconstructed, even if reunification came twenty years before.

At last the key catches in the lock and the door swings open. The music is more insistent, someone in the building is having a party. Cool sheets though, she's tired enough to sleep through anything. She plods past the mailboxes, turns and yelps when she sees a figure sitting on the lino-clad stairs. Fabrizia, Merle recognises, in one of her handstitched dresses. She's full of something, her eyes are rolling in her head and all at once Merle understands that the party is in her house, the house she shares with the Musician, his house. There will be no stopping tonight. She should have let the taxi go on, let it drop her wherever she ran out of money. Where would the Fotograf's professionalism be then, if she was clipclopping lost in one of the outlying schemes?

Merle squeezes past Fabrizia and up the stairs, round the small landing, up the next flight, her hand skimming the smooth wooden banister. Suddenly it's as though she's buffeted by a surge of air, a current, and she stumbles and slumps back against the wall, and inside her head she's spiralling round and round, until someone catches her and holds her up. She opens her eyes and there's the Fotograf, and instead of his camera he's holding her. That strawberry blond hair that's been darting across her peripheral vision for the past week is here, in front of her face. Merle has never looked in his eyes before now, this moment on the decrepit stairs. He kisses her so hard that she thinks she's falling again, dreaming again maybe, of open skies. It feels as if she wants him like she's never wanted anything else in her life before. Not the Musician, not anything. Then she hears the shrill of a voice, Frau Mildenberger, fed up with the noise, leaning over the banister and screaming into the stairwell: *Schlampe, Schlampe.* And then the Musician is there, all drugs and ego, and the Fotograf's hands are on her, and all their so-called friends come out to stare, waiting for the scene, waiting for the violence.

They drank whisky on their first date, in a corner Kneipe near the old cemetery on Auguststrasse. The mirrored gantry glinted like a jewellery box. Vodkas and hand-labelled schnapps, liqueurs infused with herbs and gold leaf, absinthe greasy with dust.

I don't like beer, she said.

That's a shame, he said. Everybody drinks it, here.

Not me.

She spotted five familiar bottles all in a row, and asked the Kellerin for whisky, *ohne Eis, ohne Wasser*. He changed his order to match hers, and by the time two hours had passed the Kellerin was bringing the bottle to the table and their tally had rounded the corner on their beer mats.

I'm going to be famous, he said, sometime after their fourth.

Why are you telling me, she said.

Because we shouldn't be drinking a blend when there's a malt right there on the shelf.

Bright daylight wrenched her from sleep the next morning. She was lying on a couch, a blanket covering her. There were no curtains over the windows. She saw a bird flit by, followed by another, heard the pulse of their wings. It might have been five in the morning; she assumed she was in the Musician's apartment. There was a green ceramic stove in one corner of the room. She wobbled through to the kitchen, the tiled floor grimy under her bare feet, found a glass and ran the tap until the water turned cold and clear.

Too drunk to fuck, she said when she saw him standing in the doorway.

Not any more.

She put her glass down and leaned back against the worktop. The Hinterhaus was derelict, she noticed, looking out the window just before he touched her.

They met again to see a performance in a bar near Warschauer Strasse, intense boys with laptops, circuit benders hunched over a bench. He arrived first, had a whisky waiting for her. The barmaid looked disappointed when Merle sat down beside him, flicked her cloth at the table as though Merle had brought dust in from outside. She'd been going to drink wine, decided it didn't matter. He was the most handsome person in the room. She remembered echoing shouts and footsteps as they walked through the Oberbaumbrücke afterwards, the rattle of the train overhead and a fight breaking out on the U-Bahn platform.

When he flew back from meeting the record company, he brought bison grass vodka from duty free. They went to the old squat on the corner of Torstrasse, pushed the boarded-up door open and called out hello. There was no one home, or perhaps no one lived there anymore. They climbed the stairs, right up to the top of the building, sat there deep into the warm night, smoking and passing the vodka between them.

This is it, he said. My dreams are coming true.

When he smiled at her she felt as if she was falling down a rabbit hole. It started raining but they stayed to finish the bottle, then edged down the dark staircase and across the floor of what once had been an office. This time they could hear snoring, discern vague shapes under the blankets on the old folding beds.

Entschuldigung, she whispered.

Sorry, he said.

They ran through the rain hand-in-hand, their clothes plastered to their backs, her face washed clean of make-up. Back to his house; she hadn't seen hers for days. When her flatmate asked if she should advertise the room, Merle said yes.

He played a gig at a secret club to celebrate. Not so secret, she thought, watching the audience. In amongst the artists and the wasters, the poets and the gap year girls in head-to-toe American Apparel, were the kind of people who furnished their Mitte apartments with contemporary art, who shopped in the designer stores. Trustafarians, people who'd do anything to stay young and hip, to keep from feeling like sell outs.

At the after-party she could see his eyes flit round the room, his gaze sliding over a collage of flesh; collarbone, thigh, back. Denim loose and low on hips, jersey draped over nipples. If she wasn't there, he'd be all over them. Even with her there, perhaps. She'd seen it in the way he was on stage; like someone who'd climbed higher than he thought he could and was tottering there, magnificent. The next day the restaurant where she washed dishes fired her for coming in late, still drunk.

A week later she came home to find the bedroom door closed, a pair of wedge sandals kicked off in the hallway. Size 39, she saw, hunching down to turn them in her hands. Soles worn but the turquoise leather still hard enough to blister. She placed them neatly by the skirting board. He walked into the hallway naked, saw her sitting on the couch reading. Merle didn't bother looking at the girl, liked him less for the way he hustled her out the door. The girl's sandals caught on the metal edges of the stairs. Merle listened as the sound grew fainter, heard the front door slam.

There didn't seem any point in having a row so they got drunk instead, a roguish barman with a thick black beard bringing them glass after glass of Grüner Veltliner in the bar along the road. She ordered olives and bread, pasta with puttanesca sauce.

I've never seen you eat so much, the Musician said.

She shrugged, ran her finger across the pasta bowl and licked the last smear of sauce from it. She felt as if she was preparing for something, insulating herself inside.

He won't want to use you if you're fat, he said.

Do you think I care, she said, tearing the crust from the last slice of bread.

He's a proper fucking artist, you know.

So are you, she thought about saying, but didn't.

She'd seen the Fotograf at parties, hadn't remembered his name. There had been an exhibition in an empty flat on Mehringdamm. Clusters of grainy stills pinned to bone white walls: a vendor at the Türkenmarkt, counting sweet potatoes and clementines; one of the Ukrainian corner girls, with her tight corset and camera-shy patrons; the Austrian woman from the Backerei Leitner, prising Vollkornbrot from tins. Field recordings playing behind black curtains. Merle couldn't remember ever speaking to him.

Why me, she said. She wasn't really an immigrant, just passing through.

I don't know, the Musician said. Because you're with me.

OK, she said. I'll do it.

Now she's sitting on the Fotograf's bed in a small room in a fourth-floor apartment in one of the workers' palaces of former times. The windows are open and she can see the tips of the trees green and swaying. The hairs on her arms rise with the breeze.

So, Stockholm or Wien, he says, grinning so that she feels it inside, wants to gorge herself on him.

There are traces of bruising on his face, on his knuckles too. She wouldn't have imagined he could fight, he seems too slender, too pale. But then she missed most of it, hunched on the landing, clutching a black eye. Bad luck that the Musician got to her first.

What do you reckon, she says, thinking of waterways and islands, then of dark corners and tarnished gilt.

Wien's cheaper.

Wien then, she says, remembering the Actionists, their excesses. Wondering if this is her last migration, or whether she'll move on again.

Rachael Boast

The Window

To those walking the river path
this morning, I have the luck of the view
while remaining invisible,
undressed behind the mood of the weather.

That would cheer you up. I can see you
looking over, waving perhaps,
trying to make out my long arms,
my long legs, the long shadow of my smile –

for you've been on both sides of this window,
seen how people stare at nothing in particular,
nothing they could put a name to;
seen how water lends itself to white cloud

to anything that's transitory – as though it's easier
to love the things that don't stay.
I'll look for your looking one day, before I
become window, become view, become rain.

What You Will

(or, Twelfth Night)

I kept my wineglass empty at mealtimes
so I might remember you in that transparency

then stole away from the house of festivity
for the silver decorations the sun creates

in the tops of the trees. I didn't think.
I became a breeze, as though a piece of heaven

had landed in me so I'd suddenly know my way:
circling the church by the floating harbour

I re-read that look in your eye, recalling
the blue boy on bread and water and the rhymes

of the hour, the moon conjoining Jupiter
among the seven hundred poems of the sky.

The North Porch

(Thomas Chatterton)

Not knowing until the moment comes
at some late hour, who you are,
or might be; raving in the Lunacy

of Ink, the night tapering, dissimilated
from papyrus, from scraps, from daily bread;
the three-fold bosses of tail chasing tail

after tail; looking out at the gospel
in capitals, level with the buttresses,
led back, time and again, to the image,

not of the builder but of his masonry;
of dream-vision, miraculous city,
the marvelous breasts of the girls in the doorway…

The Scribe's Migraine

(Ruth 3)

And so it was that morning fell open
into the shape lips might make
after a song of high praise,
or like water pouring from a jug.
But then it sets in again:
last night's lines, still illumined,
burning in the shut book of his brain,
resume their discordant tones.

Midday, and the doors he calls at close.
No share of meat with a sprig
of rosemary, no shadows
in the street, not one raised voice.
The trees shoulder the darkness
as he follows the violet paths
to where the wind moans ad nauseam
and his vision's cut with rain.

And he'll try again under candlelight,
night's rainbow, with an unknowing
closer to home than home itself
yet exiled from the home
he could have chosen. And so
it came to pass at midnight
that the man was afraid,
and turned himself: and, behold

Aldeburgh Beach

The sea takes over from human speech –
its flung rhythms seize
on what you don't know,
what you can't say,
and drown you out.

Your gaze won't reach
far enough, will skim,
give up and try again
until you say, unthinkingly –
like the waves, we disappear, and yet remain.

Edwin Morgan *interviewed by* Russell Jones

23 May 2009, Clarence Court Residential Home, Glasgow

What was it that drew you to science fiction poetry? Why did you want to write it?

I think it may be that it comes out of an interest in narrative, unusual narrative, in exploration. The idea of exploration, I think, applies both to poetry and to the physical exploration of the world and the universe and I think that one way in to it, one defence if you like, is that it sharpens… widens your awareness of kinds of life, kinds of place quite different from your own. Some are actually there, some are possible, some are perhaps impossible except in terms of arts. I found that whole area of exploring what has been, and what has not been, very interesting.

About realism in science fiction – do we need to have reality in science fiction poetry for the reader, to help them to understand what's going on and how to read it?

That's a difficult one. I think there must be some connection, though it may be very far fetched or unusual. A science fiction poem which doesn't really work is usually one which has no connection that you can see in any reality at all… it wouldn't help if it did. My own poems are trying to extend what we all think of as being reality; perhaps each time you manage to write a successful science fiction poem you are helping to extend the area of reality and saying to people: 'Are you quite sure this is not real? Perhaps it is.' Controversy and discussion come in to science fiction poetry a good deal. Although I'm knowledgeable up to a point, I'm not an expert by any means… but I like very much the area of doubt and controversy in science. A sense of change is very important; a lot of the poetry I've written has tried to emphasise that, and to say that if you were to discover, perhaps, some fossil or some human remains which are different from what we have in life today, it may alter our idea of what life is. The *Star Trek* series drew on that idea quite a lot. *It's life, Jim, but not as we know it!*

Yes, exactly!

It's a very attractive idea [laughs] and very possible. Quite possible, when you think that animals have senses that pick up things that we don't pick up. You wonder if you'll ever be able to understand what it's like to be a fly or a shark. If an animal can manage to experience things that are important to it, perhaps just to survive, then we may be able to look at that and think about it because we have to be able to survive ourselves... though we're not sure of the best way of doing that.

To present an alien world we must speak in an alien tongue in a way. How do you think that this relates to your work? I'm thinking of First Men on Mercury' which seems to point towards the idea of introducing alien tongues as a way to learn from each other.

It's actually very far-fetched because Mercury is much too hot for any kind of tongue we'd recognise... and I just did that to get away from the ubiquitous Mars background. But yes, I think it is essentially true that so far as we know, no one has tried to communicate to us from other places, which is strange in a way. It may mean our senses are not receptive to the things being sent out to us. They might have wavelengths which we don't get, we don't catch. And if so, could take a lot of time for that to be understood.

But I think it's partly just what part of writing poetry does, it's got to interest people somehow and it's very often the interest of working out 'Why is it spoken like that?' or 'Why is it written like that?'; 'Do we work out anything about ourselves from that?'. And is there anything really alien, or are we meant to educate ourselves to make it less alien, to become really involved communicators? If so, we haven't done very well so far.

Communication is important both for the sciences and for art and I like the idea of extending what people say about communication. Bees! Bees, dancing! The way that bees dance as a way of communicating with each other is not sound, it's motion. We don't do that to any big extent but we can understand what they're doing. And so I think that we ought to fill in the whole picture if we can and begin to see what kinds of communications are possible and perhaps, well, perhaps impossible. Who knows. But I don't like the word impossible, I'd like to say that things are more difficult or are in early stages rather than saying that they're impossible.

The poet also communicates through form; the form of the poem, for example your concrete poetry. You play a lot with conventions of form and break some. Do you think that there's any particular place for this experimentation in science fiction poetry?

The experiment is just experiment – it may be successful, it may not. It may not lead to anything very much at all. Or it may be a kind of key to open a huge door. It's important not to close the gate on things that are not understood yet – but could possibly be understood. One may be enlightened by science and scientific experiment, and this can also be done through language and through extending what we think that language can do. Any one language cannot do everything. We can learn from other languages and perhaps extend the possibilities of English (in our case). This idea has caught on quite well – a lot of the people who are interested in science fiction are interested in what it can do with words, with language. Language is one of the ways of making it both new and interesting and acceptable.

Science fiction sometimes has a reputation for not being as 'deep' as other kinds of literature. And thinking about your readers, do you think that you have a different kind of reader for science fiction poems as opposed to the rest of your poems?

No. [laughs] Well, there are people who are so obsessed by science fiction that it's all they read. I've come across people like that. If you've been to any of these science fiction conventions, er, you come across wild-eyed nutters who think of nothing else. Another type of reader might not think my science fiction poetry is really poetry, that it's something separate and not so good. I don't know about that. I've thought about it myself quite a lot. I think there probably has to be… not a hierarchy, but a range, a scale of kinds of poetry. At certain places and at certain times, people might want to read poems which are very scientific and rely very much on highly scientific vocabulary which is hard to understand. And there are other poets who are moving towards fantasy and I think there's very good poetry in that area too – science fiction without the science, if you like. In terms of readers and enjoyment, fantasy poetry has a good place. Fantasy goes into the area of myth, mythology. Who knows if the great myths of history actually have any truth to them. People argue about King Arthur and the Knights of the Round Table… perhaps somebody can show that they really did exist, perhaps they left records which we can decipher some day. So I think that fantasy is not something that's totally out in the cold. I think it's something you can make use of and perhaps sharpen and extend in various ways and if you think of it, any of the older poetry like the poetry of Milton, or Spencer, or Dante, Virgil, these are all, in a sense, fantasy poems. Though it depends on what your belief is: Dante wouldn't thank you for being called a fantasy writer [laughs] but to most people *The Divine Comedy* is a kind of fantasy, a very wonderful fantasy. It's the same with *Paradise Lost* – if you know the Christian background of our civilisation you take it as a poem about things that happened, although it's all in the imagination.

Today, fantasy has latched on to science fiction in many ways and you don't have to be ashamed to be found reading a fantasy novel… If it's well done, if it's well written. [In the nineteenth century] Edward Lear and Lewis Carroll were writing fantastic poetry and fantastic prose… Lewis Carroll was a very well-read man, and there are a lot of great things in *Alice's Adventures in Wonderland* which are based on scientific ideas – speculations about time and about just what we are meant to be doing in this world. It's very hard to pigeonhole things as we'd like to. That's probably one of the reasons why *Alice* or Lear's poems have lasted as well as they have. They're still being read so there must be something there that's quite real. There's not much reality about *Alice*, but enough to say 'Let's see more of this, let's get more'.

Your first collection of science fiction poems was Star Gate: *why did you decide to release a collection of science fiction poems? You hadn't before, so what had changed?*

I think people have wanted to get away from the rather stereotypical poetry of the white-coated scientists in the laboratory, it's been a kind of cliché: if you don't have a white coat, and pouring something from one vessel into another, you're not a scientist. But we're living in the cyber age now, and it's time to extend that in to other writing. It's very difficult to think of reality as simply a one-way process. In fact, an advanced scientific novel today would be quite hard to read because the ideas themselves are difficult to understand – and that would be putting a clamp on your feet. If you want to publish your book and get people to read it, it must somehow be on their wavelength. If Einstein had written fiction… I don't think he did, did he?… well, it would have been very difficult to understand. But his ideas were so important that people ought to see them somehow. Watered down, no doubt, made simple. There has been something going on now for quite a while and it's gradually being brought into writing, into creative writing. Whether a person who's actually a scientist would write a better novel than an ordinary novel by someone with a basis of science, I don't know. But I think that if you take the scientific interest too far then it goes out of the real wavelength altogether and readers can't do very much with it.

'Bawr stretter' – I don't know if I pronounced that right – 'Bawr stretter' from 'The First Men on Mercury' recently appeared on a Scottish Poetry Library badge and on a booklet and on their wall. Your science fiction poetry holds intrigue and importance for both academics and readers out there; people who are interested in poetry. Why do you think it is that your science fiction poetry is so popular, and is it an important part of you as a poet?

People enjoy 'First Men on Mercury' partly because it does tell a kind of story, and the narrative's quite strong… there's a place for work that puts its characters into very unusual or difficult or almost impossible situations, and people enjoy that. Science fiction has come to a wider audience through films rather than books. I'm not sure this finishes the book but if people are going to stop reading books then they have to get their science fiction in another way and I suppose they're going to get it visually, in seeing a film. And that can be very powerful, like in Tarkovsky's *Solaris*. It has a good story, you want to know what is going to happen next, and it also has a lot of scientific interest. You want to know just what would happen if… if certain things did happen, what else would follow on from that? So it appeals on different levels: it's exciting, it's beautiful in parts, it's frightening in parts, and it gives you ideas you have to grapple with somehow. Talking about communication: can *anything* communicate? In *Solaris* it's an ocean, a body of water, which is trying to communicate with human beings. At first you think, no no no, not really, but it makes you wonder if there is perhaps nothing which is incommunicable. And this is an idea which I put about quite a lot. 'Nothing not giving messages' – one of my statements. I believe that as we've learned more and more about science and about the world, more and more things that seemed impossible have been found to be just possible.

Yes, quite like your poem about the apple and the idea that nothing not giving messages; maybe we just don't understand the apple's message.

Yes.

Which links back to the idea that if aliens are trying to communicate, that we just don't have the way of understanding…

Of course, the idea of aliens and what they do, what life they lead, can be frightening. And this is why some people don't want to get into it too much, because they think that it's probably rather bad for you to allow your fantasies to become too black and like to think of good aliens rather than bad aliens, because it could be either! It's as well to keep your mind open in that respect: good aliens might be both very clever and ethically moral beings which we could learn from. Perhaps we are very primitive compared to some beings elsewhere; we just don't know yet. Whereas they could be out to destroy us, and in writing you want the story to be exciting – you'll have conflict, you'll have wars, you'll have various kinds of terror, and sometimes you say, 'No, don't do that,' but people will always do that; it's something to write about. There's plenty of violence in the great writing of the past. So you can't rule it out, but in science fiction you've got to find some way of making it exciting; it might be very dangerous, you've got to say it's dangerous. But that's just one way of doing it, and after all it is just a story, it's not biography or autobiography.

Most science fiction films about aliens seem to be about invasions, don't they? Although in Star Trek, *for example, the humans tend to get on well with the other alien races and they learn from each other and their morals… as a way of surviving. And surviving is something which, to me, seems very important to your science fiction poetry.*

It would be very important to understand if anybody is sending out messages, – we want, if possible, to understand what they're saying. Perhaps they're sending us warnings about this and that and we don't know what that warning is, but it might be very important indeed. And we ought to keep thinking about this.

In your poem 'Scan Day', you talk about the experience of Computerised Tomography and I was wondering, when you had the CT scan, did you feel like you were in a science fiction story, going through those kinds of machines and those kinds of things?

Hmm, hmmm. Yes. I don't know, I don't really know the answer to that.

Well that's fine, we can just move on! Do you have any advice for me or other people who are writing science fiction poetry?

Well, it needs to fit in with yourself and your own life. It's got to be something that really gets you going; vibrates in your mind, vibrates in your heart in some kind of way… If there's something you've read about in the papers or in a book or seen in a film and you think to yourself, this is very interesting. I must think about this and perhaps extend it in some kind of way and write about it – and not be inhibited by anyone saying to you, 'This is impossible, it won't happen'. Perhaps it will. Openness is very useful. You want to cut off your connections with all the existing historical novels or early science fiction – keep it in your mind, in the background, but find something that really interests *you*, whatever it might be. It might be time, it might be evolution. And keep hammering away at that until you get a good form for it. It's a matter of form as well as ideas – what I said before about language is very important: language and form. You want to read quite a lot and only keep the things that interest you particularly, things that chip in with what you do yourself, what you're thinking of, experiencing. And you'll find something, I'm sure, that really does excite you. You may want to emulate some other writers who interest you particularly, I don't know, it might be Ursula Le Guin or Ray Bradbury. There are many different types of novels, different types of poet too, and I expect it's quite good to read quite a lot. Not necessarily to copy – put yourself to school on other writers. Know what you're doing, and to say, 'I like that, I can do something with that'. And read on, and fit it into a gradually understood background.

Ian Duhig

Poem Beginning with a Line from Timothy Donnelly's 'Poem Beginning with a Sentence from "The Monk"'

Storage of this nature should, but can't be infinite,
yet there is, at least, an infinite number of infinities
signing in and out of Hilbert's chain of Grand Hotels:
dirty-weekending falsidical paradoxes called Smith,
veridical paradoxes on their umpteenth honeymoon.

Infinities concertina in mirrors of infinite narcissists.
I myself have always lived in a time outside time
since bagging that plenary indulgence as a child,
serving mass nine first Fridays in a papal jubilee.
Everything can seem like a good idea at the time,

The first moon still inside us all hosts other worlds:
our pasts and futures Ptolemaic matryoshka dolls,
paradoxical mothers beyond all Orthodox theology,
wombs soft smiths for forging guilty consciences,
each unique, a snowflake in hell, as original as sin.

Silence of the Lamb

My own first experience thus predisposed me
to deal with silence in religion primarily as evasion

— Diarmaid MacCulloch, *Silence: A Christian History*

Like the Witch of Walsingham's Chapel,
'Monk' Lewis' imaginary convent flew
to trap Maria 'Mad' Monk in Montreal,
rechristening itself as the *Hôtel Dieu.*

She swore to seeing nuns and priests
trample their rape-victims like grapes,
tossing the bastard fruits of their lust
on their dead mothers in quicklime pits.

A priest made us laugh at my school
with such tales of Protestant bigotry,
mad as those the new boy would tell
of Christian Brothers, Sisters of Mercy.

The Scripture of the Jade Pivot

(Taken from the memoirs of Lady Hong)

When he began to study *The Scripture of the Jade Pivot,*
the prince's disposition changed, and he became terrified
of certain objects, no longer daring look at the characters
for 'jade' or 'pivot', or at the jade pivot charms given to him
at the May festival to ward off calamity. From this time on
he was terrified generally of the sky, and of the characters
for 'thunder' and 'thunderclap'. He murdered the eunuch
Kim Han-ch'ae, and brought his head impaled on a stick
to shock and terrify in turn the ladies of his father's court.

When the king summoned his son to Sùngmun-dang Hall
he seemed to know all the facts and be testing the prince
as to whether he would confess. On that particular day,
he replied to one question, 'It relieves my pent-up anger,
Sire, to kill people or animals when I'm feeling depressed.'
The king asked why this was. 'Because I am hurt, father,'
replied the prince. 'I am hurt because you do not love me.'
Then he confessed the exact number of those he'd killed,
court maids, blind fortune-tellers, translators, physicians.

It was about noon when the prince asked me to come
and suddenly a great cawing flock of magpies rose up,
surrounding Kyongch'un-jon Mansion. What an omen!
When I arrived at the Toksong-hap Audience Chamber,
I found him leaning against a wall, frightened and pale.
I thought that he would fly into a rage at the sight of me,
but he just said, 'I have a feeling that they will let you live.

Then, astonishingly, he suggested we run away together.
We both wept on hearing the horses in the courtyard.

When the king finally took the decision to kill the prince,
striking the floor in his anger, I can't describe the sight.
Why did the prince not resist going into the grain box?
At about four o'clock in the afternoon of that July day
it rained heavily and the thunder rolled across the sky.
The grain box was shut and buried beneath the grass.
This was proper, something I would not dare to criticise.
I was spared to be responsible for the royal grandson.
My gratitude is so deep that it is engraved on my bones.

The Imaginary Municipal Gallery Revisited

1 The Imaginary Municipal Gallery

A research assistant on Malraux's Musée Imaginaire,
Jorn first conceived of his own imaginary museum,
the embryonic Institute for Comparative Vandalism;

his imaginary book *10,000 Years of Nordic Folk-Art*
noting folk topology's snaky roads, spirals, mazes,
revolutionary cycles, identical exits and entrances;

his imaginary exhibition called *Die Welt Als Labyrinth*,
a three-day derivé co-ordinated with walkie-talkies,
would escape its gallery to rebuild the city in words –

'The Labyrinth that is the Production of Situations'
built by Queneau's rats for the purposes of escape,
to be food for real snakes in this imaginary garden.

2 'The Wall that Went for a Walk'

Alchemist Goldsworthy
turns poetry to stone
while 'drawing' a wall
like Klee with rock ink.

Winding wind-mortared
up hill and down Dale,
each with a language
as hefted as its sheep:

hole turns to *smoot*,
footing's now *found;*
tie moves to *through,*
cap becomes *crown*:

a Tom Snout dream
marries Storm King;
limestone and wind
for their golden ring.

3 Earnshavian Cento

Fly is the Spirit of the Labyrinth incarnate.
The Minotaur has a sense of humour: didn't
it erect a DANGEROUS CORNER AHEAD sign?
Would YOU trust a signpost in the Labyrinth?

4 Curator's Choice

Like one of his pickled farm animals,
this loiner artist now divides himself:
on one side, a brainless gilded calf:
beneath our skin, a diamante skull.

The other half? A calf's head rots,
St Luke incarnated in a glass box,
as flocks of unconverted maggots
digest his gospel message. Watch:

one by one, they are born again:
under diamond eyes, albs burst
to show off new black hair shirts;
as their stained-glass wings open,

one by one our saved souls rise
towards the electric blue skies
of the built-in insect-o-cutors.
Now that really created a buzz.

Carol Farrelly

The Glass Lift

Robert wished the woman would go – go and leave them in peace. She stood there in the corner of the lift, a shopping bag slung over her gloved hands, face in half shadow beneath a crimson headscarf, and eyes large with watching. Robert grabbed at his son's good arm and drew him closer. It was always the same with women, whether a wife or a stuck-up busybody in a department store lift. They demanded a man prove himself – show he was a mindful father.

The spindly arrow above the doors juddered and a bell tinkled. First floor. Gentlemen's clothing. An old man in a trilby hat tottered past them, wandering into the forest of flared denim and sheepskin jackets. The woman stayed in her corner, eyes as bright and fierce as a newborn's.

'Almost there, son,' Robert said. 'Just three more floors, eh? Then you can pick yourself something. Maybe one of they model plane, eh? Or a Scalextric car?'

'Maybe,' the boy mumbled, not looking up, wriggling his arm free of his father's grasp and digging his hand into his pocket.

Danny was nine years old now; he thought himself too old for holding hands with his Da. It was only natural. And a small mercy, really. Robert had never enjoyed holding his son's soft, hot hand. It made him nervous – the cling of such smallness in his large, callused hand.

The lift doors shut again. Robert glanced across at the woman again. The eyes had grown darker and the lips thinner – an expression he recognised only too well. Mary favoured that same expression. The woman was staring at the plaster cast on Danny's left arm and the yellowing bandage attached to his cheek. She was probably imagining the trail of purple stitches knitted underneath. None of your bloody business, he wanted to mutter. Nobody's bloody business but his and Danny's. It had had been the same at the Infirmary last week, nurses and doctors with clipboards clicking their shiny Parker pens. – How did it happen? Was nobody watching your son? Did nobody see the guilty car? Not even the boy himself? – Pen-pushing busybodies. More like the bloody police than doctors and nurses nowadays. And parents were always the first suspects, especially the fathers.

Danny, however, had said nothing. Robert had to give him that. His silence had been immaculate.

'It's pay day, son,' he said, patting his wallet pocket. 'It's pay day and your Da is going to treat you.'

The woman tilted her head forwards, as though his speaking, and his speaking so soft, gave her permission to come out of her shadows. The amber eyes narrowed above the long nose. Robert stared back at her without blinking. She sniffed and retreated back into her scarf's crimson shade.

Ting! Second floor – bedding, curtains, kitchenware. The lift doors slid open and the woman sidled past them and glided off without a backward glance. More interested in her eiderdowns now, of course. The husband was probably a banker or a lawyer. Heath's bloody three-day week would make little difference to his fat wallet or her generously fed purse. Never mind the wee wean with the broken face: now she had switches of curtain to clasp and measure. Robert rested his hand on Danny's shoulder.

The lift doors closed and it was just the two of them.

'Do you mind that story about the glass lift, son?' he asked.

The boy stayed silent.

'Do you hear me, Danny? It's not that long ago we read it.'

The boy waggled his head as though trying to shake a wasp from his hair. 'Don't remember,' he said.

The boy's reflection wavered in the silver doors, like a body disappearing under water.

'You remember – by that writer, you know, who wrote about the chocolate factory. And that poor lad, who didn't even have a bed to himself. Found a golden ticket wrapped around a chocolate bar. What was the lad's name…?'

Robert knew Danny still had the dog-eared book crammed into his bookcase; he had spotted it the other afternoon, while the boy was at school. He liked to potter in the boy's bedroom sometimes, flick through whichever book lay by his bed, pick up the comics he kept on his shelves. It must have been less than a year since they'd read the glass lift story together, during his last ever leave. Danny liked stories and Robert understood that. He could admire that in a son—the wanting to escape, to sail, to fly.

'Do you remember, eh?'

Danny shrugged his shoulders and continued to stare at the floor.

Robert sighed through his nose. The boy had been like this for the last month now – ever since his mother had gone into that maternity hospital, the posher side of Glasgow. Or maybe it had happened earlier. Sometimes Robert wondered if Danny had started behaving funny three or four months since, as soon as he'd quit the army, since they'd all been living together in the house, father, mother and son, every morning and every night. Maybe it had started even earlier than that. Danny was not a forgiving boy – he blamed his Da for being away so long. It was all the mother's doing, of course. A brooding wife. A suffocating Ma. The tour of duty in Belfast was the last straw, she'd said. The army or us, she'd told him. Even though nearly every other bugger in the country was striking or earning only three days' pay. Even though there was no earthly sense in it at all. He'd become another man on Civvy Street, that choking, spit-bowl, fag-end street. He had let her turn him into a man with a janitor's pay.

Not that it had made any difference. She still brooded. A couple of weeks ago it had been the joke he made about her belly, plump as a partridge. He had only said it to make light of her lying in the hospital bed, to let the pregnancy seem fine and healthy. The doctors were forever fussing. 'So much older', this second time around, they said. 'We have to be careful.' They whispered of the previous miscarriage and the haemorrhaging. They danced that word, 'haemorrhaging', around her bed and he saw a coven of fairy-tale witches. 'She's safest here,' they said, frowning at him, as though it was his doing alone she was pregnant, as though she had not caressed and kissed and persuaded.

Robert gazed down at the boy's blonde cap of hair.

'Do you want an action man?'

'No,' the boy frowned.

A few weeks before the hospital, she had brooded when he suggested that Danny might join the Cadets. Teach the boy the survival skills. Work some muscle into his wee brain. That conversation had ended with her pouring a bowl of piping lamb stew into the sink. So much for his playing the interested father. Always best to keep your eyes, ears and mouth shut. Be the three little monkeys all in one.

'How about some more Meccano?' he asked.

The lift shuddered. The lights flickered and dimmed. Danny's open mouth rippled in the silver wall.

'What's happening?' he asked, looking up at his father for the first time.

Robert glanced up at the twitching arrow. 'You're all right, son. It's nothing to worry about. It'll be another bloody power cut. You need to take a candle and matches wherever you go nowadays, eh?'

The lift stopped. The little arrow sat midway between the three and the four. There was just the flickering of a lime-coloured light. And a slow undergrowth of sound. The purr of electricity. Far-off music. His son's shallow breathing.

'No, Dad! It's all still alive out there!'

Robert couldn't help but smile. It was a long time since he'd heard that word, 'Dad'.

'We're stuck, Dad! The lift's stuck!'

'Keep yourself calm, son. Always remain calm. We'll just press this button here, see.' He reached out and pressed the red alarm button. 'They'll get us out in five minutes, you'll see.'

He stared down again at his son's tousled head of hair. His hand hesitated above the softness.

'We should have taken the stairs,' Danny moaned, clasping his plaster-cast hand inside the good one. 'Mum would have made us take the stairs. It's always safer, she says. And she's right, see.'

Robert's hand fell. It was a rag-doll head of hair. A head in need of a good comb and a wash. The boy had no idea how to keep himself. The mother did everything for him. No safety in that. Only dependence. A noose of apron strings. All those years he'd spent away from them, she'd ruined the boy. His every second bloody thought was hers. Safe. Everything had to be safe. It was no way to nurture a man of the boy. Spoiled, cringing, no fire in his wee belly. As though the world were all cosy, hemmed-in streets. All quiet, cooing rooftops and gold-topped milk bottles sitting by bowls of cornflakes. Never bottles rinsed clean by lads not much older than Danny himself, creamy milk bottles turned into petrol-black bombs on back-room tables.

'See?' the boy persisted.

'We're safe where we are,' Robert muttered. 'Have a drop of patience, will you?'

Danny didn't look up.

'If Mum was here, I wouldn't be stuck –' Danny began to gasp for air. Robert heard the missing swell of words. I wouldn't be stuck here 'with you'. Ungrateful wee sod. And so prim. Always 'Mum'. Never Ma. Never Da.

'Aye, of course! If she was here, everything would be milk and honey, wouldn't it? All sugary porridge, eh?'

The boy's face paled and Robert remembered again. He thought of the first afternoon his wife went into the hospital. Danny had come home from school and Robert had opened the front door to him. The boy had sensed something was wrong in that moment: a defensive sweep of eyelashes upon his small, flushed cheek. Dad never opens the door – that's what he'd thought. Later, after he had explained and Danny quietened down, he made the boy a clumsy dinner of burnt sausages and watery mash and sent him early to bed. No bedtime story. No mother's goodnight kiss. That was how the boy had seen it, no doubt, but Robert had feared more comparisons. He would read the wrong story in the wrong voice; his lips would bristle the boy's cheeks.

Robert dug his hands into his anorak pockets. His fingernails pressed against a caked handkerchief ball. The boy was too young to understand. Men had to carve out a safe place for themselves.

'Listen, son…' he said.

Danny reached up and stabbed at the red button three times with his stubby finger.

Robert stared. His chest tightened. His son couldn't bear to stand inside the same four walls with him.

'Stop it!' he yelled.

And it was that same claustrophobia in Danny, that impatience of claustrophobia that had caused the accident.

'I've already pressed the alarm. Just have some patience. Everything will be fine.'

The boy stared up at him. 'You said that about Mum,' he mumbled.

'What?'

'You said be patient and wait. You promised you'd take me to the hospital and let me see her. But you haven't. You won't!'

Robert's heart clenched again. 'You'll see her soon. She just needs a wee bit of time on her own.'

They'd said it to him only yesterday, still the 'threat of miscarriage'. Total bed rest. 'No excitement.'

'Is she dying?' Danny asked, his eyelashes dark and clotted.

Robert swallowed. 'Course not, son. She's fine. She just needs to save her energy for the new wean.'

'But she's been in the hospital ages now! And I've still not seen her. She'll think I don't care!' Danny paused, his wet eyes widening with the idea. 'She'll hate me!'

'Stuff and nonsense! She wouldn't want you seeing her in the hospital.' Robert reached down and patted the boy's shoulder. 'It would be too hard for the pair of you. That's why.'

'But I want to see her! And you said! You said you'd take me to see her.' The boy faltered; he gestured towards the plaster cast. 'Before the accident.'

Robert stared. 'Aye, well – maybe you would have seen her, eh? If you hadn't been so daft.'

Danny blushed.

'Your mother can't see you like this… Your hand all in plaster. Stitches on your face. She doesn't need any more upset.'

The boy stamped his foot and his face flowered red as the poppies Robert weeded from the school playing field. 'I want my Mum!'

He'd said those same words the morning of the accident. A whining mantra. He'd driven Robert to distraction. For a moment, just one moment, Robert's right hand had clenched and it was then he'd turned to Danny and told him they would go for a drive to the seaside, to Millport and Crocodile Rock. Anything, for his son to look up and give him a smile. His own Da had taken him there once as a boy, before he'd buggered off one summer night without so much as a goodbye. He'd skimmed stones across the water and spoken to Robert of his wanderlust and he had not understood at the time. Only six years old. But he had liked the yawning feel of the word on his tongue. 'Wanderlust.'

And the promise of sea and ice cream had seemed to calm Danny that morning. Robert told him to wait on the pavement, like always, while he reversed the car out. He checked his rear and side-view mirrors, like always. And he saw nothing, only a still street and close-up, sunlit tarmac. He had seen nothing.

Robert glanced again at the fidgeting arrow still stuck between the three and the four.

He closed his eyes. He heard the sound again. The muffled thump of wheel and metal felling nine-year-old bones. He felt the pressure of Danny's rag-doll limbs as he rammed his foot down on the brake. The boy's fault. He knew not to hang around the car. Robert had drummed the dangers into him. Lucky he hadn't been killed. That was what he'd told him afterwards. How many times had he told him? The world wasn't safe. Stay on guard. Carve out your space and hold it.

The boy pressed his right hand against the lift door and began to whimper.

'Stop it now, Danny! Do you hear?'

The boy pressed both hands now against the doors as though they might have magic in them and his touch might open them and he might run off into his ready-made chocolate factory.

'Let me out,' Danny cried.

He began to pummel the doors with his good hand. Imprints of his small outspread palm flowered upon the metal and faded, over and over. He stood back. They both watched his reflection waver.

'I hate you,' Danny shouted, as he turned, pressed his back against the wall and slid down into a hunch on the floor.

Robert's chest clenched. 'Go on! Hate me, then! You wee mammy's boy!'

The boy hugged his arms around his knees and began to sob. Robert said nothing as he watched. He wondered if the tears stung as they trickled over the trail of stitches, the bruising work of needle and thread upon his son's pink, elastic skin. Danny's mother would not wonder. She would scream if she saw that small pillow of cheek, bound to be scarred for life. He couldn't bring the boy to the hospital looking like that. 'What kind of father can't be trusted with his own son?' Better than no Da, though. At least he always came home again. He stayed, even though sometimes he didn't know how.

Tools clanged below and voices trilled, tinny like a lullaby on a far-off radio.

'You'll bring on another bloody accident, if you carry on like this.'

'Good!' the boy yelled.

Robert looked down at the boy's burning face and the curls of blonde hair, which flicked up under his ears. The moth-shaped bruise on his tiny cheek seemed larger now; the shrinking bandage no longer hid the biting zip of stitches. And the plaster cast had grown thicker and mustard yellow. The sunlit tarmac flashed again in the mirror.

'Good? What do you mean by that?'

Danny looked to the floor. 'Good,' he mumbled again.

'You want more stitches, do you?'

'I –'

'What?'

Danny stared up at him, his cheeks blotched with tears.

'Spit it out!'

Danny's eyes flared. 'I'm glad the accident happened.'

Robert's heart withered. 'What?' he asked.

'I got to the hospital.'

Robert stared.

'I got near Mum.'

The lift shuddered. The tarmac flashed again in the side-view mirror. And there was a flick of blonde hair. A slice of pink cheek. Robert frowned. No, that was wrong. There was only a still street. Only sunlit tarmac. Empty. He had seen nothing else.

He grabbed at the boy's arm. 'What you saying, eh?'

Danny pulled and stepped backwards.

'Nothing,' he gasped. 'I just want to see my Mum.'

'The day of the accident…'

Danny's mouth trembled.

'You waited behind the car?'

The lullaby of voices grew louder. Danny said nothing. His face was a blank–a matchstick-man face, impossible to read. But Robert saw it all. Even now his son squirmed to be free from his hands, as though they were a vice, as though he was the cagouled stranger Mas warned their children against.

'You hate being with your Da that much?' he asked.

Danny shook his head and stepped backwards.

The voices were just beyond the doors now, a gossip of lullabies. He could already see the scarved woman who had been in the lift earlier. She would be there, waiting, her eyes large and amber again. Danny would run away from him into her talcumed arms. Away from the turpentine arms of a janitor, a has-been soldier, a no-good father.

The lift stopped again. The bell tinkled.

Robert stretched out his hand towards Danny's bruised face.

'Son?'

'Don't!' the boy whimpered.

The doors gasped open. Danny darted out through the fluttering crowd. Robert's hand fell.

Diana Hendry

The Greenhouse

Before my father gave her away,
On cold sunny days
My sister shut herself in there
With a bag of apples
And her library book –
An historical romance wrapped
In cellophane sticky as semen.

It was a sun trap in winter.
On the slatted bench
Big terracotta pots of tomatoes
Gave off their particular musty stink,
Fattened and turned from green to red.

Abigail's Garden

Grows children, chaos and, of course, a sapling
Apple, tiny and daring its very first blossom.
Walk past and a shock of energy's sparked off
As if it's in the grass or maybe fed
On *Miracle Gro*. So it's no matter that
The fence is down, the gate half off – there's
Too much growing going on to give
To everything its due. Here's a sandpit,
Trike, a mini trampoline. Now bluebells
Have landed. No wonder next door's clematis
Is wanting in or that old ginger cat,
Terrified of metamorphosis or worse,
Wants out. He's bagged a patch of common
Sun-warmed pavement and is nodding off.

The Romantic Couple: A Fantasy

They ask me the way to the river.
She's from Latin America. There's a century
of flamenco and fiesta in her face. On the corner
of a Scottish street castanets start clacking
in a swirl of petticoats. He's a professor.
His shoulders are bent with the weight
of philosophy. In the cool of a medieval
courtyard he murmurs Cervantes.

They ask me the way to the river
and such a longing comes over me
as if Segovia had picked up my heart
and used it to strum 'Humorada'.
Take me in! I want to say. *Take me
into your lives. I'm kith, I'm kin!*
I show them the way to the river,
set off in the opposite direction.

O my dear lost loves,
ask me again the way to the river,
the way to anywhere,
the way to the past.

Andrew Taylor

Just words writing

In a 1949 letter to John Steinbeck, John O'Hara judged that F. Scott Fitzgerald 'was a better just plain writer than all of us put together. Just words writing'. That this evaluation was something of a minority view, certainly while Fitzgerald was alive, is made clear in a new account of the life and times of *The Great Gatsby*'s author, *Careless People: Murder, Mayhem and the Invention of* The Great Gatsby, by Sarah Churchwell, Professor of American Literature and Public Understanding of the Humanities at the University of East Anglia. H.L. Mencken, never one to resort to nuance when hyperbole would do, declared that *The Great Gatsby* was no more than a 'glorious anecdote' in which 'the story is obviously unimportant'; another review judged the book to be an incoherent mix of 'melodrama, a detective story, and a fantastic satire, with [Fitzgerald's] usual jazz-age extravaganza adding his voice to the mental confusion'. Even posthumously there was no respect, for the Episcopalian minister who officiated at Fitzgerald's funeral was reported as saying that 'The only reason I agreed to give the service, was to get the body in the ground. He was a no-good, drunken bum, and the world was well rid of him.' Three days after Fitzgerald's death in 1940, at the age of forty-four, the *New York Times* offered an editorial summary of the author and his greatest work: *The Great Gatsby* 'was not a book for the ages, but it caught superbly the spirit of a decade… here was real talent which never fully bloomed'. These judgements, foolish as they are from the vantage point of literary historical hindsight, nevertheless encapsulate an interesting critical problem, one that is not unique to Fitzgerald but which he exemplifies at an acute pitch. What is the relationship that the anecdotal has to the creation of literary art? How does the raw material of a culture – its addictions, its corruptions, its ephemera – help us understand how literature works? The contemporary critical notices of *The Great Gatsby*, and of its author, argue that Fitzgerald was unable to rise above, or beyond, his quotidian moment, to stay sober for long enough to create art 'for the ages'. Churchwell's book wants to reject such an evaluation, but as a model of literary history it forces the reader back towards the anecdotal, investing it with a significance that it often cannot sustain.

Within American letters maybe only Herman Melville has suffered the same degree of critical disdain followed by canonical enshrinement as Fitzgerald, though on the evidence of the half-a-million copies of *Gatsby* that are sold annually (with more predicted this year on the back of Baz Luhrmann's excessive film adaptation), the author of *Moby Dick* still has a long way to go to match the curricular and cinematic reach of Fitzgerald's tale of lost illusions amidst the corruptions of capital. Melville and Fitzgerald continue to provoke academic interest and have offered themselves as challenges for literary history: how does one account for their contemporary neglect? To what extent is their writing in tune with, or antagonistic to, the contours of a particular cultural era? How far can literary history itself explain, or account for, literary art? Successive biographers have combed over the details of both men's lives, and both have also recently had the novelisation treatment (with Jay Parini's *The Passages of Herman Melville* and R. Clifton Spargo's *Beautiful Fools*), as if conventional literary history now needs to be supplemented by the possibilities of fiction.

For the academy, the scope and focus of literary history remains an area of debate. How useful are our short-hand periodisations of, say, 'the early modern', 'High Victorianism', or 'modernism'? Can any intellectual or aesthetic judgement ever be safely drawn within such parameters, despite our insistence on the period as the central historical concept of our system of literary education? Literary history needs to be clear about the kinds of claims it can make for a chronological span that might be both distinctive and yet, inevitably, part of a larger continuum whose genealogy is impossible to circumscribe. In a recent article in *New Literary History*, Eric Hayot notes that periods 'instantiate more or less untheorized and inherited notions of totality' through a 'typology of wholeness' whereby 'any single period theorizes an entire apparatus or background against which its own essence emerges'. Hayot is rightly suspicious of the ways in which academia has institutionalised the study of literature around a series of chronological limits that produce our familiar narratives of literary history. What would happen to those narratives, he asks, if alternative sets of parameters were to be deployed, through a more transnational approach to literary study, or via a stretching of the historical period? 'What we call Victorian literature might look quite different from the perspective of a Victorianist than it would from that of an imaginary scholar of the 1850–1950 period', he suggests. Hayot's is a useful reminder that literary history, maybe necessarily, imposes its own borders of coherence. As Henry James noted of life's endless permutations, while 'relations stop nowhere' it is the writer's 'exquisite problem' to 'draw, by a geometry of his own, the circle within which they shall happily appear to do so'. The happiness is never unalloyed, however, for the 'perpetual predicament' of sequestering diversity for the sake of artistic shape is the author's constant companion.

Perhaps this nagging anxiety over the artificiality of form can be alleviated if the literary historical focus tightens to a smaller unit of chronology, say a single year. This approach has yielded very successful results in the form of James Chandler's *England in 1819: The Politics of Literary Culture and the Case of Romantic Historicism* (1998) and Michael North's *Reading 1922: A Return to the Scene of the Modern* (1999); 1922 is also the subject of Kevin Jackson's more recent day-by-day study *Constellation of Genius: 1922: Modernism Year One* (2012), a useful almanac of who was creating what in a year that is retrospectively held up as culturally remarkable, witnessing the publication of Joyce's *Ulysses* at its start (February) and Eliot's *The Waste Land* towards its end (October). There are other contenders for modernism's most significant year – 1910 (according to Virginia Woolf) or 1915 (according to D.H. Lawrence) – such that the accolade itself becomes a kind of sophisticated literary party game. Jackson presents the roll-call of 1922's credentials, but his book shies away from any kind of conceptual narrative that might help us navigate our way around and through its daily update of cultural highlights. If a reader wants to think about how episodes within a single year of modernism might generate, or respond to, structures of the public world into which works like *Ulysses*, *The Waste Land* and E.E. Cummings's novel *The Enormous Room* (published in April) were received, North's book remains unsurpassed. It asks us to think of modernism 'as a social fact, as part of the lived experience of a reader' of Joyce's or Eliot's texts. (This focus on the materiality of modernism is something I'll return to.) North's is an instance of literary history that works hard to avoid the dangers of totalisation, as described by Hayot, by looking beyond canonical and national models for inspiration: while the chronological period is precisely defined, the geographical purview is expanded to remind us of the transnational and multimedial flow of ideas during this tumultuous moment.

Walking the streets of New York in the summer of 1922, the narrator of *The Great Gatsby*, Nick Carraway, finds himself attracted to a new form of visual experience, one that seems to transform the epistemological possibilities of the city. 'I began to like New York,' we read, 'the racy, adventurous feel of it at night and the satisfaction that the constant flicker of men and women and machines gives to the restless eye.' The incessant mobility of the urban scene, its transient, exciting possibilities, are brought into focus around the word 'flicker', with its echo of 'flick', an early slang term for cinema that the *OED* dates from 1926, the year after *Gatsby*'s publication, but a word which one imagines may already have been circulating within popular discourse before then. 'Flicker', then, marries the conditions of city living to the optical reception of cinematic frames to evoke the possibility of a transformed, rearranged experience: the materiality of film begins to augment modernity's vocabulary of perception. Sarah Churchwell's book is exemplary in bringing the reader into a world in which literature and cinema rubbed shoulders. Long Island, to where the Fitzgeralds moved in 1922, quickly became the home for prominent members of the New York film industry before it decamped to the more favourable climate and cheaper real estate of California. Churchwell tells of dining invitations from Gloria Swanson, of riotous parties with directors and movie stars, and of the scandals that such hedonism would produce. Occasionally, though, this leads to some odd synchronies: 'On 2 February 1922, the same day that James Joyce published *Ulysses*, the director William Desmond Taylor was found dead in Hollywood, shot in the back'. It is not entirely clear why this link between a key moment in European modernism and a sordid murder on America's west coast is being made, other than to remind the reader that high art and low designs can happen somewhere in the world simultaneously. More troublingly the sentence encapsulates a structural flaw at the heart of this book and the awkward literary history that it performs. Whereas North's account of 1922's rich matrix of elite and popular cultural practices is alive to the ways in which textuality itself is transformed by serendipitous collisions (Fitzgerald's use of 'flicker' being one small, but telling, example), Churchwell's focus remains squarely on events and personalities, on episodes within Fitzgerald's life and in the wider social scene that might have had an influence on the themes and characterisations of his most famous book. So we learn that William Desmond Taylor had in fact been born William Deane-Tanner, and his reinvention, social ascent and violent demise offer themselves inevitably as a narrative prefiguring of the plot Fitzgerald is about to write, as if Taylor's death on the day of *Ulysses*'s birth somehow makes the story available for America's own gestating piece of high literary modernism. This is both tantalising and incidental, but Churchwell is keen to force the larger significances. 'America', she writes, 'was invented out of a desire for rebirth, for fresh starts. It was the place where a man could be the author of himself, reinventing himself as an aristocrat, but somehow these stories of renaissance kept ending in murder'. *Careless People* is the biography of a year – 1922 – and of what the Fitzgeralds did during it. 'This factual account', Churchwell writes, 'is threaded through with Fitzgerald's fictional account in *The Great Gatsby*. The two mirror, reflect and amplify each other, a kind of two-part invention in which fact and fiction are in contrapuntal relation'. But this relation is never adequately theorised, and the book's collage of incidents, gossip, and capsules of social and cultural history (on, for example, financial scandals, prohibition, car crashes, or the composition of Gershwin's *Rhapsody in Blue*) have the cumulative effect of pushing *The Great Gatsby* out of focus, as if overwhelmed by the anecdotal. Contexts spin and proliferate such that there is little time to think about the novel, as literary art, anew. Churchwell claims that 'Meaning can be salvaged from the wreckage of experience: accidents may reveal a pattern, a composition of sorts, if we look closely enough', but the risk in this is that the accidental is transformed into literary history, a narrative of explanation that expects to see through randomness to find design.

The Taylor killing, for a time 'the biggest murder story of 1922', is overshadowed in the book by another documented case of violence, the slaying of an adulterous couple, Eleanor Mills and the Reverend Edward Hall, in New Brunswick, New Jersey, in September 1922, 'a murder mystery', Churchwell writes with a degree of journalistic exaggeration, 'that held all of America spellbound'. The shootings of Hall (married to an heiress to the Johnson and Johnson fortune) and his mistress, the choir singer Mills, filled the newspapers for weeks. Churchwell writes of how the murder scene itself became a location for ghoulish tourism (and inevitable commercial opportunity), and hers is the most comprehensive account we have of the manifold failings and corruptions of the police investigation and the legal process that followed. The bodies had been carefully arranged after death, with Hall's arm cradling Mill's head, and Mills's hand placed on Hall's thigh. Love letters between the two had also been strewn around both corpses, leading to wild speculation about the identity of the perpetrator(s). One of the large claims Churchwell makes for her book, in its retracing of how *The Great Gatsby* came to be written, is that the Mills-Hall case provided Fitzgerald with a plot arc and a set of character types that might not have been available to him elsewhere – or indeed imagined by him autonomously. She writes: 'it is my contention that this remarkable story [the Mills-Hall murder] amplifies and enriches the story of *Gatsby* in many more ways than have yet been appreciated. Everyone knows that *The Great Gatsby* offers a connoisseur's guide to the glamour and glitter of the jazz age, but the world that furnished *Gatsby* is far darker – and stranger – than perhaps we recognize'. This is a strained claim to make, on at least two counts. It is impossible to demonstrate the impact of the, at the time, celebrated criminal case on a piece of literary art, in the absence of any explicit commentary by Fitzgerald to help us. The plot possibilities of adultery and violence are not so unusual that Fitzgerald would have needed an historical source to guide him through their contours. Moreover even the most cursory reader of *The Great Gatsby* surely cannot help but be aware of the 'darker – and stranger' world that it depicts; its peculiarly American tragedy depends on Fitzgerald's sober dissection of the glamour that Churchwell assumes is all that we register. Yet even in 1922 Fitzgerald's friend Edmund Wilson was telling his readers, in an acute literary judgement, that 'Fitzgerald is romantic, but also cynical about romance; he is bitter as well as ecstatic; astringent as well as lyrical. He casts himself in the role of playboy, yet at the playboy he incessantly mocks'. What Churchwell wants to establish, at the start of her book, is the existence of a widespread but naive reading that can be redeemed by the dark historical facts that are subsequently marshalled for us. Even here, though, there is a degree of slippage, as the Mills-Hall contention gets modulated to 'a notorious double murder [that] might well have worked its way into Fitzgerald's mind': the link between historical incident and literary production is less causally secure. This more tentative approach to the problem of how events might transform themselves into literature seems more sensible (even if one is tempted to wonder why knowledge of the murder case matters *at all* to our appreciation of the novel it is supposed to have influenced). But Churchwell's book insists on narrating the history of the murders, the incompetent investigation that followed, the widespread interest the case attracted, and the bizarre personalities it spawned. Running alongside the biography of Scott, Zelda and *Gatsby* in 1922 are the meticulously researched stages of the case, and the two narratives at times are asked to recognise each other in unconvincing ways. For instance, during their investigations the state prosecutors revealed that the police were looking for a light green car in connection with the murders. Churchwell follows this procedural detail with a moment from the novel whose significance is claimed, denied, and then asserted again:

> At the end of *The Great Gatsby*, the police will also be told to look for a light green car in connection with a homicide. A tiny detail, too small to qualify as circumstantial evidence, it is probably just another coincidence, but coincidence has its own beauties. Even such small historical symmetries can suggest there are patterns all around us, reminders of how expansive the possibilities truly are.

Literary history of this type cannot quite accept the possibility of contextual irrelevance (or 'coincidence', in Churchwell's more benign formulation), for 'patterns', a word as we've already seen she likes to invoke, must be discerned in order to hold history and fiction together. Such symmetries are not, to my mind, generative of hermeneutic expansion, but on the contrary they construct reductive mechanisms for the reading of literature in which the discovery of contextual detail becomes a key to all mythologies.

The reader expects a moment when the key is turned and the significance of the murders for the novel is made explicit. When it comes, the effect is distinctly underwhelming, as Churchwell considers the collision of real-life and fictional killings:

> At the end of *The Great Gatsby*, there are three explanations for the deaths that litter the Long Island stage, all motivated by adultery: the aristocratic

Southern wife did it [Daisy]; the inadequate working-class husband did it [Wilson]; and it was a case of mistaken identity. These are also the three possible explanations that were offered for the murders of Eleanor Mills and Edward Hall. Fitzgerald's story about possibility is capacious enough to grasp all three possibilities. The creative process makes the murders of Hall and Mills look unneeded: the story has been set free to fly into fiction, transposed into a different key, but audible in echoes and harmonic shifts, transfigured from the wretched to the beautiful.

To admit that the writing of fiction might not require the contextual mapping that *Careless People* has so painstakingly established is undermining to its thesis and, of course, true. Although Churchwell wants to hold on to the idea of the historical trace, the vagueness of its echoes, shifts and transpositions in fiction might make us wonder if its presence is all that significant in the first place. Moreover there is something a little too neat in the final clause's conversion of historical wretchedness into fictional beauty, as if Churchwell's prose itself has become infected by Nick Carraway's inclination to aestheticise away the material ugliness of conspicuous consumption in his narration of Gatsby and Daisy Buchanan's doomed romance.

Churchwell cannot resist the temptation to tell her story through the kind of narrative omniscience often to be found in fiction. Writing of Eleanor Mills, sitting in her New Jersey home reading a popular romance, we are told that 'At thirty-four she didn't look old enough to have teenaged children, or to have been married for seventeen years. She was wearing her favourite dress, dark blue with cheerful red polkadots, and was avoiding the housework, as usual, to finish the book. She always lost herself in romances, but this one was special: it had been given to her by the married man with whom, for three years now, she had been having an increasingly passionate affair.' There is an easy confidence about this sketch. The phrase 'as usual' signposts an authorial knowledge the reader is required to accept, as does the detail that Mills 'always' succumbed to the pleasures of romantic fiction; and polkadots that are 'cheerful' draws attention to itself as a descriptor that might not seem out of place in Fitzgerald's fiction. While this can make for engaging writing and vivid characterisation, much has to be taken on trust for we are often never sure how, or from where, such scenes are sourced. There might be something appropriate in this blurring of empirical evidence and narrative embellishment in a book dedicated to American literature's most precise evocation of exactly this phenomenon, yet Churchwell's combination of dogged archival work and often portentous summary ('Everything about Gatsby is synthetic, including his gin – everything except his fidelity'; 'History might be a stowaway, but we need the ballast it provides') results in a curious study that strains at the plausibility of literary history and does little to add to our understanding of how *The Great Gatsby*, as a piece of literary art, works.

When Churchwell turns her attention to the novel, leaving aside the welter of contextual possibilities that are being ranged around it, she often demonstrates the kind of acute critical sensibility that makes one wish that the book's texture had preoccupied her more. The unexpected, surreal clauses that litter Fitzgerald's prose ('the orchestra is playing yellow cocktail music'; 'A tray of cocktails floated at us through the twilight'; 'he dispensed starlight to casual moths') strain against an ostensible realist aesthetic that only ever has a tenuous hold over the book. The sensory disruptions that result draw attention to the sensibility of our narrator (why does Nick choose to describe the world in this way?) and to a culture that seems to have freed itself from the standard etiquettes of perception. As Churchwell notes, 'Voices in this novel don't speak, they are "glowing" with sound. Colours nearly always suggest scents or tastes as well: Gatsby's house is decorated in rose and lavender silk; his tear-jerking shirts are in coral and apple-green and lavender and faint orange. Music has a tendency to liquefy: silver scales float over a body of water called the Sound while banjos "drip" their tinny tunes'. Nick's status as participant, observer and retrospective chronicler of the events of 1922 is central to our continuing fascination with this novel. 'His occasional bouts of silence and aphasia', as Churchwell points out, produce the kinds of delicate epistemological problems that sustain multiple re-readings. The issue, she suggests, 'is less that the accuracy of Nick's narration cannot be relied upon than the fact that he cannot always be relied upon to narrate'. There is an easy symmetry to this formulation that seduces, and I'm not entirely convinced that its emphasis is accurate, but the claim that 'Nick is a romantic in the Keatsian sense: he thinks untold stories are lovelier' seems just. Yet Nick does also tell stories, ones that may be lovelier through his embellishment, and this sense of a narration that self-consciously mediates the terms of its reception occasionally gets lost in Churchwell's reading. Two examples of this will suffice, both figured around the perception of women.

At the end of chapter six of the novel we are treated to Nick's account of Gatsby's recollections of a meeting he had with Daisy five years prior to the book's chronological frame:

> His heart beat faster as Daisy's white face came up to his own. He knew that when he kissed this girl, and forever wed his unutterable visions to her perishable breath, his mind would never romp again like the mind of God. So he waited, listening for a moment longer to the tuning-fork that had been struck upon a star. Then he kissed her. At his lips' touch she blossomed for him like a flower and the incarnation was complete.

There is something overheated about these sentences; it is writing that teeters on the edge of absurdity in its insistence on transcendence, on simultaneous loss and incarnation, and on the purity of Daisy's romantic fulfilment (in which her whiteness continues to signify). Churchwell quotes from, and paraphrases, this passage, and follows it with the assertion that 'Nick distances himself from this "appalling sentimentality"' – a phrase that Carraway does indeed use to judge the encounter he has just relayed to the reader. Yet this begs the question: whose appalling sentimentality is actually on display here? Churchwell assumes that it is Gatsby's, faithfully relayed by his narrator, but there is every reason to wonder if the romantic over-investment is in fact Nick's, in which his desire to see beyond the crass materiality of the novel's protagonists creates the heady language of sentimental fiction. Churchwell demonstrates a literalism here – one at odds with her awareness elsewhere of Nick's problematic status – that fails to take into account the ways in which Nick's narrative point of view continually reimagines the story in the act of telling it.

This reluctance to consider the way in which Carraway fashions a narrative to suit his own psychological obsessions finds its most telling form in Churchwell's account of the death of Myrtle Wilson, Tom Buchanan's working-class lover who is killed by Daisy in a hit-and-run car accident. At this point in the novel, as Churchwell points out, Nick is reliant on newspaper reports and the official inquest to tell his story. 'Nick is now narrating as a reporter', she writes, 'and so can tell us of things that he didn't see at first hand'. While this is indeed the convention that the novel assumes, I'm not sure that it precludes the reader from attending to the language that Nick chooses to deploy in describing the death scene to us. Churchwell assumes reportage, when in fact there is an uncomfortable descriptive emphasis that might tell us as much about Nick as it does about the event itself. Here is the passage:

> Myrtle Wilson, her life violently extinguished, knelt in the road and mingled her thick dark blood with the dust.
>
> Michaelis and this man reached her first, but when they had torn open her shirtwaist, still damp with perspiration, they say that her left breast was swinging loose like a flap, and there was no need to listen for the heart beneath. The mouth was wide open and ripped a little at the corners, as though she had choked a little in giving up the tremendous vitality she had stored so long.

The contrast with the ethereal, non-sexualised kiss between Gatsby and Daisy quoted above, in which bodily compulsions are replaced by spiritualised ones, could not be stronger. Daisy's whiteness, something insisted upon in the book and with complex resonances of ethnic, class and sexual legitimacy, has its counterpoint here in Myrtle's 'dark blood' and her insistent, because violated, corporeality. It is as if Nick's reporting of the death performs a kind of moral reckoning, in which female sexual desire is punished for its temerity. Nick's general discomfort around women – the relationship that matters most to him in the novel is with Gatsby – finds its most gratuitous articulation here. Because we are structurally locked into Nick's embellishing imagination, it is impossible to determine the provenance or accuracy of his account. Yet it would seem to be a naive reading indeed that doesn't consider the ways in which the vocabulary choices that Nick makes might be both distorting of the scene and clarifying about him.

Careless People follows on the heels of a book published last year which, like Churchwell's study, thinks of itself, in part, as a biography of a book. Michael Gorra's *Portrait of a Novel: Henry James and the Making of an American Masterpiece* tells the story of James's *The Portrait of a Lady* (1881), and, again like *Careless People*, it fuses life and fiction in narrating the cultural, literary and biographical influences that coalesced around the composition of its chosen novel. There is much to recommend in Gorra's work – he is alive to the literary genealogy of James's text in a way that Churchwell rather underplays in the case of *The Great Gatsby*, and his mastery of the biographical detail of a long writing life is impressive. What Gorra and Churchwell have in common is a desire to rethink what literary criticism can do and who it might be for. In the prologue to his book Gorra is explicit about this: 'Most people don't read criticism, not beyond the length of a review. They read narrative – that's why biography is so popular'. The resort to narrative over criticism, as a way of wrestling discussion of literary texts away from the increasingly specialised language of the academy, is not, in itself, a regrettable move. Public understanding of the humanities may be well served by books that are jargon-free and construct their literary histories around a single object (the novel) or a single year (1922). Yet there is something dispiriting if, as professional literary scholars, we have given up on trying to explain how a piece of literature continues to frustrate and fascinate through its linguistic challenges, and why it can never be reduced to its contextual components. The best criticism does this, admitting defeat in the face of art but willing to return again and again to art's provocations. John O'Hara's sense that Fitzgerald's genius was of 'just words writing' speaks to an aesthetic brilliance that continues to defy our attempts to describe it.

Patrick McGuinness

Two Stations

for ZW

Bruxelles Congrès/ Brussel Kongres

It's now an out-take, a special number of a station,
closed at weekends 'to help disengorge the network':*
but still the trains pass through it, run it through,

reminding us how quickly these days we produce Oblivion,
how fast we waste, how obsolescence more and more
comes neck and neck with what it obsolesces

and soon may come before it. It probably already has.

* Found poetry from the SNCB spokeswoman.

Bruxelles La Chapelle/ Brussel Kapellekerke

This is the deadest of the *gares-fantômes*: deadest
because so freshly dead: renovated first and then sealed up,
embalmed in €uros, a skatepark sarcophagus of graffiti.
In this undercountry, it's not ghosts who pass through us,
cold crossings of mortality, but we who pass

through them, sleeving the spectres with our bodies.
The buskers have moved on, the commuters moved away,
the *waffel* stands have climbed above the ground:
all are blinking in the light that they half-knew,
returning from the half-light they knew best.

Doug Johnstone

There are Easier Ways to Kill Yourself

Harry heaved himself over the wooden groyne that split the beach. Too old for this. Where was that stupid dog now?

He looked up and stopped. He'd seen plenty of weird things on Porty beach over the years, but this was new. Fifty yards away was a beaten up Honda Civic, facing out to sea.

He squinted into the low winter sun and reached for his hipflask, took a hit. Sainsbury's own brand blended scotch, all he could afford until pension day.

There was someone in the driver's seat of the car.

Harry looked around. No one else in sight. It was too early yet for the school run and the young mums pushing buggies. He hadn't been able to sleep – no surprise – so he'd shrugged his clothes on and headed out with the dog. Speaking of which.

He spotted Buster at the water's edge, rolling in something.

'Buster!'

It better not be another dead jellyfish, that stench hung around for days.

'Here, boy.'

The dog sprang up and headed over. Harry patted him and sniffed. Nothing pungent.

The car engine revved, high and long.

'Come on, boy.' Harry trudged towards the car, weary feet kicking up sand. How could sleeping pills make you so knackered yet not help you sleep? He should go back to the doctor, but he couldn't face that look, as if he didn't have the right to insomnia, even after all this time.

As he got to the car he noticed the tyre tracks in the sand. Looked like the guy in the council's sand-cleaning tractor yesterday had forgotten to replace the concrete block between the prom and the beach. The Honda had squeezed through the opening. What would the driver have done otherwise, just gone home? Harry thought about that.

He looked at the driver now. A young lad, still in his teens. About Jack's age when it happened. The most common age for this shit.

Harry knew what this was and felt a rock in his stomach. Everything he'd learned since Jack's death. The scab he still picked every moment of every day. This was a suicide attempt, and a piss-poor one at that.

The lad was sniffling, head down, looking at a piece of paper in his hand.

Harry tapped on the driver's window and the lad jumped. He wound the window down.

'You all right?' Harry said.

The lad stared at him, then down at the piece of paper. He handed it over, shaking. Harry squinted at it, holding it away from his face. It was an email printout. The lad had printed out bad news? Nothing surprised Harry. One time he'd heard of a jumper being pulled out the water along the firth, a laminated suicide note pinned to her coat. Laminated. He couldn't get over that.

He tried to read the words of the email, useless without his glasses. He handed it back.

'She never loved me,' the lad said. 'The whole thing was a joke, a fucking lie. Three years, what was the point?'

The lad put his foot on the floor and the engine raced. Harry had to stop from shaking his head at the puerile gesture.

'I'm going to kill myself,' the lad said.

Harry wanted to throttle him. How dare this little prick want to end it. He was in possession of his life, the greatest gift there was, the one thing Harry's son gave away. But at the same time Harry wanted to help, stop this lad making the same mistake as Jack. Harry was used to this conflict in himself. Five years working on phone lines and helping charities, he still had a double-edged reaction even now.

He breathed slowly, took his hipflask out and had a swig.

'How?' he said.

The lad looked confused. 'What?'

'How are you going to kill yourself?'

'I'm going to drive into the sea.'

Harry sucked his teeth and shook his head.

The lad was outraged. 'What's wrong with that?'

'That's no way to kill yourself.'

'Sorry?'

'I'm just saying there are easier ways to kill yourself. Hanging is most common, but the most effective method is jumping off a high bridge or building. Ninety-eight per cent success rate. Booze and drugs don't work so well, but they're easier, though you could end up alive with brain damage or organ failure. I wouldn't recommend slashing your wrists, only six percent succeed that way.' Harry looked at the lad, the car, then the sea. 'Still more likely than this.'

The lad frowned. 'What are you, a suicide expert?'

'Something like that.' Harry put a hand on the car door. 'Tell me, what do you expect to happen here?'

'Just fuck off.'

'Think you'll get trapped in the car and drown?'

'I said fuck off.'

'You haven't thought this through. Most likely the engine will stall before the water even gets over the wheel arches.'

'Fuck off!'

The engine revved as the lad threw the car into gear. Harry stepped back, grabbing Buster's collar and pulling him close as the wheels threw sand into the air and the car jolted forwards.

He had forty yards to the sea and got up some decent speed for such a crappy car. It hit the first waves with a splash of spray and the engine racing. Ploughed on into the froth but then slowed rapidly until the engine cut out and the car jerked to a stop thirty yards into the waves, the water just over the floorpan of the chassis.

Harry let go of Buster's collar and watched. Nothing for a few seconds, then the chug of the ignition turning over, not catching. A second time. A third.

Harry saw the lad beating the steering wheel with his fists but all he could hear was the shush of the waves on the shore.

The driver's door opened and the lad stepped out. Water rushed in through the door and filled the footwell as the lad stood, wet past his knees.

He looked out to sea. Oil tankers way out there, implacable. He looked at his car, then turned and looked at Harry. His shoulders slumped and he waded towards shore.

Harry looked round. Still no one else on the beach.

The tide was coming in and he wondered how much of the Honda it would cover.

The lad approached, shivering, the printout crumpled in his hand.

'Don't say a word,' he said.

He sat down on his haunches in the sand. Buster sniffed at his trouser legs.

Harry shooed the dog. 'Away, boy.'

He sat down and got his hipflask out. Drank from it and looked at the lad. About the same height as Jack, gangly too, floppy dark hair. But then every teenage boy Harry had laid eyes on since Jack hung himself reminded him of his son. Every poor kid he'd spoken to late at night on the Samaritans line had sounded like Jack.

Every teenager still alive was a reminder that Jack had chosen to die.

The lad was sobbing now, shoulders heaving, tears dropping on the sand. Harry raised a hand and placed it on the lad's back. Rubbed up and down. It felt awkward and inconsequential, but he kept doing it. Gradually the lad's breathing calmed and he wiped at his eyes and nose.

Harry waved the flask in the lad's eyeline. The lad wrinkled his nose.

'What is it?'

'Whisky.'

The lad took it and swigged, grimaced, handed it back.

Harry took another drink then pocketed it. 'What's your name?'

'Lee.'

If only Harry had had a moment like this with Jack, things might've been different.

Lee wiped at his nose.

'Don't feel bad,' Harry said. 'The odds were stacked against you.'

Lee stared at him. 'What do you mean?'

'For people your age the success rate for attempted suicide is terrible, worse than one in a hundred.' Harry smiled. 'People my age manage it one in four times. Maybe we take it a bit more seriously. You know the World Health Organisation reckons twenty million people try to kill themselves every year across the world. Imagine that.'

It was a statistic Harry found comforting. All those desperate souls, united in something at least.

'How do you know all this stuff?' Lee said.

Harry could've told him about Jack. Could've reeled off all the stats he'd learned since Jack's death, all the methods for survival he'd been trained in, how the most effective way of avoiding suicide was simply to talk to someone. Like they were doing now.

But the lad didn't want to know all that. Harry wouldn't either if he could've helped it. Jack's death had turned him into someone who cared, but he wished he didn't have to care that way.

He shook his head and stood up.

'Come on, I live along the road. I've got some dry clothes you can have.'

Lee shook his head. 'No thanks.'

Harry stared at him. 'I'm not leaving you here on your own.'

Lee looked into his eyes. Maybe he saw something. Maybe not. He got up then looked out to sea. 'What about the car?'

'The car's fucked.'

Lee laughed under his breath. The kind of thing Jack used to do whenever Harry surprised him with a swear word. He put his arm around Lee's shoulder and led him away from the beach, Buster mooching at the sand alongside.

Behind them thin sunlight glimmered off the water as the tide slowly filled the car through the open driver's door.

Laura Scott

After Christmas

Is anything sadder than a train in a siding,
seats slashed and bleeding their white
stuffing into the air of an empty carriage?

Maybe the old horse, blind to the field
around him, walking all day between
flanks of wood, cutting the earth into lines.

Maybe the man walking down the hill
playing his harmonica, wearing a new coat
made out of hair. Or maybe it's you

swilling the things you haven't done
around your mouth, like cherry stones
to be left on the side of your plate.

Bad Day

Like breaking the seal on a gull's feather,
running your fingers across the harp of grey

barbs before you pull them into oily strands.
Like finding someone else's words coming out

in lines from the side of your mouth. Like a horse
clipping the pole with the rim of his hoof,

turning his ears when the white paint chips
as it hits the support and rocks, for a moment,

before it falls to the grass. Like waiting for you
to ring, knowing my dread is cut with longing.

Bones and Lines

Time on my face,
>> not in my hands, pulling
>>> his fingers down my cheeks,
leaving his lines running
>> from my nose
to my mouth.

I knew he'd find me one day
>>> but I'd forgotten he'd come for you,
and lay his hand over your brow,
>> to thicken the skull under
>>> your skin, to draw
the boy into the air,
>> to seal the man into the bone.

Finding the Line

Give me the nerve
        to stay in this place
where light plays with truth.

Let me spread myself
        across the air
like a fan of peacock's feathers,

shaking off the dust with my
        blues and greens.
Let me think of peaches and honey,

of threads of red, veining around
        the stone, cutting
the sweet yellow flesh in half.

Let me find the line's balance
        under my foot
like that church we found in the v

of the road, with its garden
        at the front
where the trees curled like vines

and the cars roared past
        on either side,
like cars in a black and white film.

Let me draw the stillness
                from the wall
in through my fingertips

until it runs through the rays
                of my feet.
Let me find the air's ease

and remember how, up here
                grace hides
her face in difficulty's sleeve.

Rachael Boast

'My wisdom? Scorned as chaos': Rimbaud's Carson

The appearance in September 2012 of a selection of Arthur Rimbaud's prose-poems, known as *Illuminations,* adapted to verse by Irish poet, novelist and musician Ciaran Carson, marks a turning point both for those interested in Rimbaud's work and for the ongoing exploration into the task of creating 'versions' or 'adaptations' from another language. *In the Light Of*, published by the Gallery Press, is a gallant response to Rimbaud's prose-poems of the 1870s not only because Carson adapts them into verse but because of the ingenuity of the technique by which he does so.

The language of *Illuminations* is a language of dreams and visions which goes about unveiling, exploring and delighting in the shifting worlds it moves between. Carson is well placed to have published these versions owing not just to previous renditions of, or references to, Rimbaud in *First Language*, *The Alexandrine Plan*, and *Letters from the Alphabet (Opera Et Cetera)*, but to a clear similarity of poetic intent that in all likelihood has drawn him to a poet like Rimbaud in the first place. Much of Carson's work, like Rimbaud's, belongs to a tradition of what could be termed 'illumination' and goes further into that tradition than is normally the case. It would be misguided to attempt to pin down meanings in this sort of work, or to look for closure: such poetry makes designs on our sense of order and proposes a re-vision through a disordering, or, put another way, a defamiliarisation of perception. True to his word, Carson's *In the Light Of* employs a technique recognisable, in the way it makes language unfold in unpredicted utterance towards a form of illumination, as an exemplification of lyric faith. Which is to say, poetry is a means by which we can access what we don't know we know.

Illuminations is also infused in the tradition of coded imagery prevalent in alchemical and cabalistic discourse, with which Rimbaud was familiar.

His form of 'illuminism', which is, generally speaking, a concoction of such traditions, always adapted by poets to suit the contemporary setting, was inherited from writers such as Eliphas Lévi, Michelet, Balzac and Hugo, and revised in accordance with his ars poetica, emphasising how the *voyant*, the seer, contributes to social progress. An interest in codes carries well into Carson's versions, as one might expect from publications such as *Opera Et Cetera* where code is employed as a central motif throughout the book. And of course, 'code' owes itself to 'codex' – a block of wood split into leaves for writing on – an ancient book, one in which perhaps all dreams and visions are written, even in Alexandrines.

Illuminations was printed fortnightly in *La Vogue* between 13 May and 21 June 1886 and attributed to 'the late Arthur Rimbaud'. When a full length edition of the poems appeared some months later in a limited print run of 200 copies and with a preface by Verlaine, the few who did buy the book were informed its author was in fact alive and well in Asia, late for an appointment at the barbers perhaps. Rimbaud was not a man who could be easily pinned down.

It is interesting to note that Graham Robb's biography has no entry for 'Alchemy' in the index. That he skips over the subject, so crucial to an understanding of Rimbaud, raises many questions. At the same time it says a great deal about the manner by which something enters into common parlance and is acceptable to it, or is discouraged, in any given age. We have to look to Enid Starkie, decades before, to brush up on the basics. Robb does, however, allude nicely to the keystone of Rimbaud's prose-poem-parade when he suggests that the rapid shifts of perspective and fleeting impressions, for instance in a piece such as 'Les Ponts', entail that 'nothing lasts long enough to mirror a personality' – which is perhaps why Carson, taking his cue from Italo Calvino, retitles the poem, 'Invisible Cities'. It is also worth noting that the antecedent to *Illuminations* was a short series Rimbaud had collected under the proposed title, 'Études néantes' ('Void studies'), poems which, in the spirit of musical études, went beyond the temptation to convey any direct message.

The coded language of illumination is wonderfully effected in the dream-vision, 'Aube'. Placed twenty-second in the sequence, perhaps by Verlaine to whom the manuscripts were given, or by Gustave Kahn, editor of *La Vogue*, Carson, however, places it first in 'Act One' of his versions, thereby setting it up as a thematic statement. In the poem, the boy-initiate figure unveils a goddess whom he then, in a perverse or subversive act of tribute, runs after, covering a great distance between scenes rural then urban and back to rural, returning to her an armful of lifted veils. We might presume, not only from the title (which translates as 'Dawn'), connoting the morning star, and from references in some of the other *Illuminations,* such as 'Villes', 'Being Beauteous', 'Vies', and 'Fleurs' (as well as in the collected poems), but from the tradition to which this kind of imagery belongs, that the goddess is Venus.

'Aube', as dream-vision, is of course a form of the Irish genre of aisling poem. Carson retitles it 'As I Roved Out', referencing a standard folk tune opening which complements the poem in many respects. Aisling poetry has its own age-old songline, as does the old French poetic genre of *reverdie* (re-greening) which celebrated the arrival of spring, or, more generally, of spiritual regeneration – or, in critical times, of the regeneration of a culture and language. No doubt all of the *Illuminations* have their roots in the instinct that lies behind these genres; in reverie, and in what it makes accessible to the 'dreamer' who is then able to unveil some of the mysteries of life, keep in tune with them, and, in so doing, allow for them to infuse the work.

For the poem's giveaway sentiment, Carson, completely on home turf, smartly replaces 'Alors' with '*Voilà!*', stepping across the language barrier as if it wasn't there. 'Voile' in French means 'veil'; 'voiler', 'to veil'. This alteration, placed exactly halfway through the version, triply emphasises the point: working at the level of revelation ('first I heard, *now I see!*'), followed by an exclamation mark, *and* set in italics:

> Gemstones eyed my passing. Wings arose without sound.
> My first adventure happened on a path I found
>
> already littered with pale glints, wherein a flower
> spoke her name to me. I blinked. It was no known hour.
>
> I laughed to see the Wasserfall dishevelling itself
> in shocks among the pines; climbing shelf by rocky shelf,
>
> I recognised the goddess at the silvered peak.
> *Voilà!* Veil after veil I lifted from her, not to speak
>
> of how my arms were fluttering as I did so.

This is a good example of how, for the sake of the rhyme scheme, Carson explicitly adds to the original, as he does in many of these poems. Here we have the extra, 'I blinked. It was no known hour', an addition brilliantly attuned to the discourse of unveiling, as is 'climbing shelf by rocky shelf', by virtue of the way it sets up the image of an ascent towards a peak experience. As Carson says in his author's note, he changed the language of the French but then the French changed his language. The use of 'Wasserfall' accords with the original, the word being in common usage in the Ardennes at the time.

Further fun with the language exchange is the way Carson has reversed the titles Rimbaud had in English: 'Being Beauteous' becomes 'Être Belle', 'Fairy' becomes 'Fée', 'Bottom' becomes 'La Bête' (interestingly, Rimbaud himself did attempt to translate some of the poems into English whilst in London). Liberties are freely taken with other titles. For example, aside from 'Aube', 'Mystique' is 'Seer', 'Fleurs' strangely turns into 'Snow', 'Phases' is 'Phases of the Moon' and 'Génie' morphs into 'Genius'. And this is fair enough, as long as we don't presume it's Rimbaud, which it isn't – as Carson himself explicitly states in his author's note – and as long as we remember that, given his ars poetica, Rimbaud wouldn't have minded in the least; in fact, in the light of his seminal notion of 'Je est un autre' he would probably have delighted in this mature re-envisioning of his poems, something which has never been attempted since their publication in 1886, most probably because no one dared to. In a sense, these versions could be seen to present a serious challenge to the idea of authorship, and yet in so doing are, hilariously, in no way discordant with the originals and with the philosophy of their youthful author, who pronounced that 'If the old fools had not discovered only the false significance of the Ego, we should not now be having to sweep away those millions of skeletons which, since time immemorial, have been piling up the fruits of their one-eyed intellects, and claiming to be, themselves, the authors of them!'

Before looking at Carson's innovative sequencing of the versions, it is worth dwelling a little longer on Rimbaud's ideas. To do so we should return to *Letters of the Alphabet*, which references the 'Voyelles' sonnet and appears to be a version of it extended through the entire alphabet. This sequence can be described as an A to Z of a rational disordering of all the senses, putting us in mind of Rimbaud's *Lettre du Voyant*. The letter, addressed to Paul Démeny who was a friend of one of Rimbaud's school masters, was written on 15 May 1871, at the height of the disturbances in Paris shortly after the Franco-Prussian war of 1870 to early 1871, and a matter of days before French government troops marched on Paris to wipe out the Commune. Political unrest will always implicate culture and literature, and we see at the time a growing interest in 'primitive art' (a patronising term if ever there was one) and a fascination, in certain quarters, with brutality, both of which become thematic interests in French poetry. Only against such a chaotic social and political backdrop would we see arising the impetus towards grandiosity we find in Rimbaud's formulations.

Having made his first visit to the capital, the poet was back in Charleville when he wrote this letter. It is the letter of a sixteen-year-old novice excitedly formulating his ideas against a backdrop of cultural devastation and wounded national pride. France at the time was becoming obsessed with its defeat, with its vulnerability, and indeed its identity. The letter shows signs of the impact of this crisis on its author, not because he in any way dwells on the subject (aside from the poem he attaches at the start of the letter), but because of its reactionary tone, its urge towards radicalism. Exposed to the atmosphere of national unrest, and at some level experiencing a parallel crisis, Rimbaud seems to have felt that the time was just about ripe for something different, for a bout of literary upheaval and salon-cleansing. Thus, the grandeur of the ideas he expresses is a product not only of his own talent but of the conditions under which that talent was surfacing.

He writes that, 'The poet makes himself a *seer* by a long, prodigious, and rational *disordering* of *all the senses*. Every form of love, of suffering, of madness; he searches himself, he consumes all the poisons in him, and keeps only their quintessences'. This is a personal formulation of an idea that goes back a long way. Given Rimbaud is talking about poets, those quintessences therefore refer to poems, whose prima materia (or in his terms 'poisons') is to be alchemically transformed into the lapis. We might also see in the results of his application of this formulation – his actual poetic output – that he was attempting to, or rather called to, transmute not only his own experiences but the collective experience of wounded pride and social chaos and to originate the future. This then becomes one of the functions of *Illuminations*, both product of, and antidote to, a crisis of French culture.

Had their author made a stay against his customary habit of roving out in search of new terrain then he might not have bundled his poems onto Verlaine in 1875 and, instead, taken time to develop the sequencing of them. As it happens, we know that the published *Illuminations* were not sequenced by Rimbaud and some of them are probably missing and others added. The result of Carson's language experiment evokes a peculiar feeling of seeing the collection sequenced as it could have appeared had Rimbaud spent more time on it. For Carson, the structure itself is obviously as much a part of the illumination project as the content. *In the Light Of* has that look of being the book hidden within the book that was only partly opened in the first place, then abandoned to more than one pair of grubby hands before, some 137 years later, it found a new hand to write itself in.

Carson's sequencing realises *Illuminations* as a dramatic narrative with prose Intro, Interlude and Coda, between which sit two Acts of 11 verse renderings. This theatrical framing device is perfectly confluent with the thematic content of the poems, with their multiple and shifting personas. Using for the Intro the second section of the three-part poem, 'Veillées' – with its abundant references to alchemical symbols and colours – this choice, like 'Aube', presents an aesthetic statement to the effect of saying that 'I is another':

> The wall facing the spectator is a *'succession psychologique'* of cross sections, friezes, atmospheric bands and geological happenstance. Intense and rapid dream of sentimental groups of beings, of every possible character, under every possible appearance.

That Carson has singled out *'succession psychologique'* in italicised French suggests that switching between languages in this way, which he has done many times before, is a method by which we can negotiate the limits of our own language and bend them, so that language becomes an exchange between the 'I' and the 'another'. This then strengthens the aesthetic statement the rest of the book explores, the point indeed being that nothing lasts long enough to mirror a fixed personality and nothing can be pinned down to a singular independent meaning. This cast, this parade of identities, characters and places in flux, can be envisioned alchemically as a kind of torture of the metals in their crucible; the self, as it envisions the world, undergoing transformation within the containing context of literary work; the stage on which the poet acts out the process. With the heat turned up.

The Interlude (Rimbaud's 'Conté') with its Prince and Genie is an intermediary stage in this process. Aspects of this poem are developed, in Carson's sequencing, into a final climactic Paean in which the figure of the Genie, like some strange Christ, Orpheus or Merlin, reappears as a flamboyant embodiment of poetic inspiration. 'Génie' was originally placed – by someone or other – third from last in *Illuminations*. It is a lengthy piece, a great deal of which Rimbaud has probably sourced from the Cabala, with its seven Genii, adapting it to suit his purposes. It stands as an ecstatic declaration of his central concern. Carson's version of this prose-poem is placed last as the Coda, yet reads not as a conclusion but as another opening, another lifted veil. In fact, it echoes the poetic architecture of the Intro ('From the two far ends of the room – nondescript stage sets – harmonic elevations merge or mingle.') for its 'pole to castle, cape to rocky cape', etc. – this to that, or that to this – and in so doing makes it seem as if the entire book were folded round on itself, ouroboric-style. 'Genius' is indeed like an 'intense and rapid dream', one which contains some brilliant reworkings:

> Sa vue, sa vue! tous les agenouillages anciens et les peines *relevés* à sa suite.
> Son jour! l'abolition de toutes souffrances sonores et mouvantes dans la musique plus intense.

becomes:

> To behold him and behold him! All the ancient genuflections and penalties revoked at his passing.
> His day! The abolition of all sonorous and arbitrary sufferings, in a more plangent music.

Carson's version actually makes the elusive sense clearer owing to the agility of his style. The last paragraph contains several innovations which improve greatly on other existing translations, for instance, 'le héler et le voir, et le renvoyer', becomes, 'to hail him, and to see him, to return him to his echo'; 'au haut des déserts de neige': 'high in the wastes of snow' (Bernard renders this as 'at the top of the deserts of snow'); but, above all, the syntactical alterations are what gives the piece its power:

> He has known us all and has loved us all: may we learn, this winter night – from tumultuous pole to castle, cape to rocky cape, from crowd to beach, from glance to gaze, our strength and feelings ebbed – to hail him, and to see him, to return him to his echo; and from under the tides and high in the wastes of snow to follow all that he beholds: the surges of his breathing his body, and his day.

The full stop after 'loved us all' has been removed, as have several commas between the last semi-colon and colon, which effectively pushes the word 'behold' into even higher prominence. And 'behold' isn't even in the original, which has 'suivre ses vues'. Even an addition such as the 'from' in 'from under the tides', rather than 'sous les marées', increases the velocity and sense of the heightening of experience – not to mention how both the use and placement of 'from under' and 'high in', mimic 'the surges of his breathing'. These are small details but, as with each of these versions, these are the details that culminate in an illumination of sorts and are its language – as Enid Starkie notes of the poem when she says in her biography that 'Each little group of words is then intended to suggest, not the full experience, but one single flash of understanding. We do not receive the whole vision at once, but in a series of these flashes, of *illuminations,* which, in the end, force the impression into our mind'.

Viewed in the context of Rimbaud's interest in Alchemy, 'Génie' is homage to existence itself, to the 'marvellous substance', made out of all the raw and complex details of experience. Alchemy was not for him a system that could easily be relegated to the past and described as archaic but a living system that works with the reality of perpetual change at all levels of existence and could be realised through language, when language is subjected to immense pressure – and indeed, when the writer themselves are subjected to the effects of working with language in this way. The language of *Illuminations* operates at that heightened level, shared with prayer, incantation, the search for beauty and balance. Carson handles Rimbaud very naturally, working from inside the language so that the versions can still be admired and carry a charge even if the reader doesn't have the key. In the right hands, language will carry that key deep in its seam, in the 'happenstance' of its syntax and rhythm, like flashes of metal or gemstone.

There are a few surprising omissions in the sequence, such as 'Solde' (which Oliver Bernard renders as 'Clearance Sale', placed last in the sequence probably in accordance with a particular interpretation, not necessarily accurate, of Rimbaud's literary intentions post-*Illuminations*), or the classic 'Matinée d'Ivresse' (with its explicit announcement of success: 'Hourra pour l'œuvre inouïe et pour le corps merveilleux, pour la première fois!'/'Hurrah for the undreamed-of work and for the marvellous substance, for the first time!'), although in the case of the latter one suspects everything has already been said more interestingly elsewhere.

Where liberty is taken with the precision and meaning of Rimbaud's originals, we should remember that Carson has used the versions to shift or explore a poetic reality, hence his title for the book. 'Être Belle' gives us a very different poem from 'Being Beauteous', especially with the addition to the description of the being of Beauty as she 'becomes another', which the original doesn't have but which plays on Rimbaud's ars poetica. 'War' ('Guerre'), becomes an added fourth section of 'Twenty Years A-Growing' ('Jeunesse'), so named because of Rimbaud's title for the second section, 'Vingt Ans'. This is placed at the end of Act Two. There is also a rather crucial change of precision in 'Curtain Raiser' ('Parade'). Reference to a key is missing from the poem and it would have been good to have seen how else 'J'ai seul la clef de cette parade sauvage' might be rendered, as it is fairly easy to tidy up Bernard's rather uneconomical translation which misses out the reference to the (noble) savage, 'I am alone in possessing the key to this barbarous sideshow'. Carson's rendering could be said to lack the power of the rest of the poem because of being too contingent on the end-rhyme: 'And who's behind this wild curtain raiser? I, my friend.' That said, this colloquialism is still a good departure from the original. Indeed, it is necessary for Carson to set up a dissonance to the originals and assert his own poetic practice in order to avoid being sucked into Rimbaud's gravity.

The missing key is returned, nevertheless, in another form in 'Lives' ('Vies') where Carson keeps, in part two, the original French 'clef' rather than using the superfluous 'key-signature' of Bernard's translation:

> I am an inventor such as never yet was seen;
> moreover, a musician of the Hippocrene

> who has discovered something like the clef of love.
> At present, as a country gentleman, I live
>
> off my meagre lands and modest piece of sky,
> trying to rejuvenate the memory
>
> of my beggar childhood, my apprenticeship …

Previously we hear the speaker wondering what happened to the Brahmin who taught him Proverbs whilst he was living among the 'enormous avenues of the Holy Land,/the terraces of the Temple! The desert sand!', claiming he had wrought

> a stage on which to realize all the masterpieces
> of dramatic literature from West to East.
>
> I could show you untold riches. I could tell
> tales of the treasures found by you. I'd know the sequel.
>
> My wisdom? Scorned as chaos. What's my nothingness
> to the wonders that await you, and will leave you speechless?

This piece, like the fifth section of 'On the Road' (which is actually the fourth section of 'Enfance'), reads like another dramatic stage setting as the speaker reviews or imagines various lives, as it were, strolling across his alchemical mise-en-scène. This prose-poem in particular is very difficult to render from the French and anyone who tries would be obliged to have entered into the same demolition zone of the self – in which Rimbaud continuously reinvents himself – in order to build anything of worth from the exercise, for it is an exercising of the idea of I as another. This is of course true of the entire book.

The additions and alterations we find in these versions are, for the most part, a result of their adaptation into verse. This escalates them into something more rapid, light and incantatory than the prose allows for; an effect that wouldn't be possible if Carson hadn't adapted them as such, as it is verse that best draws this out from the originals where the prose somewhat keeps it restrained, for its own reasons. Behind this restraint, however, Rimbaud's rhythmical imagination, his expertise in verse forms, including the Alexandrine line, has allowed for the discovery of a hidden fanfare shadowing the prose.

Carson's overall technique is that of finding his way into these versions through sound patterning, through rhythm, through rhyme; riding on that until it creates its own spray of meaning – much like Rimbaud's discussion of a new, universal, language in the letter to Démeny: 'de la pensée accrochant la pensée et tirant.' ('thought latching onto thought and pulling.'). What gets said, gets said *through* the sound-play and results from it, not the other way around. Sometimes the line endings and enjambment are a little out of kilter in their artifice but for the most part this technique works brilliantly and is aligned with how the beauty of the language and its dancing is far superior to any message the poems might convey. The message is in the music, the measure, in the sound and syntax, and how those devices interact with the codes and symbols of Rimbaud's mysticism.

In the Light Of is a homage to beauty and inspiration. Venus returns again in the poem 'Snow' ('Fleurs'), this time in the coded guise of the rose – alchemical code for the perfected work. 'Snow' is one of the most stunning of Carson's re-workings, its consequent end-rhyme enjambments working brilliantly with the layer-on-layer of Rimbaud's rich images:

> … Pieces of yellow gold strewn slantwise
>
> over agate, tall piers of pernambuco wood
> supporting domes of emerald in the interlude
>
> of bouquets of white satin sporting on ruby sprays,
> surround the water-rose's delicate display.
>
> And like a god with huge blue eyes and arms of snow
> the sea and sky pull towards the marble terraces
>
> great crowds of white roses rising in crescendo
> as forever young forever strong they grow and grow.

The overall effect of Carson's language experiment and rapid syntax in these versions is indeed like the water-rose's delicate display. Such a display has little to do with 'authorial intent' as both those words become by the by in the context of illumination and of its language; instead it abandons the quest for having anything to say, as such, any meaning to express, and for any meaning-conditioned certainties, such as the one Madame Rimbaud was inhabiting when she asked her son what it all meant. His response: *it means exactly what it says, word for word. Comme ça.*

Simon Pomery

Music as a Gradual Process

I'm trying to clarify what it is
I'm doing: pulling back a swing to release,
observing as it comes to rest.
I'm turning over my father's hourglass
watching the pink grains of sand, with interest,
as they fall through a telephone in a miniature case.
I'm running to the ocean's edge, the fizz
of outstretching foam, to listen to the waves
as my feet disappear, waves as in 'the seas',
as in 'length of sound', 'sound wave', best
on a hot day naked with my girlfriend, which will pass
gradually, extremely, as the coast
will erode. It is summer. There are bees
moving slowly over the rocks. I can hear this.

A Gift of Silence

I hear my father's gift of silence,
coming home to find the coal room
was now a music studio. The charcoal coldness,
the smell of soot in smudged air,
the scrape of the bare floor when he shovelled coal,
the skin-coloured walls, had given way to sound-
proofing panels, carpety smells, the back window open
on trees and tinnitus, and further,
leaking brown water out of a mouth in the moor,
the low rumble of the stream invisible;
a gift of silence I would shatter
with drumming, white noise, feedback –
the freedom of a son striking out on his own,
the love of a father who lets him strike.

Pendulum Music

```
S               F               S
i i              e e            i i
l l l           e e e          l l l
e e e e      d d d d      e e e e
n n n n n   b b b b   n n n n n
c c c c c   a a a   c c c c c c
e e e e e e e c c e e e e e e e
c c c c c      k      c c c c c
n n n n n                n n n n n
e e e e                    e e e e
l l l                        l l l
i i                            i i
S                              S
```

Rodge Glass

There's Always Arizona

You put the earphones into your ears while still looking for your keys. You find them in your jacket pocket, where you left them. There's no mystery here. Then you check your bag for the second time, count the papers inside, and zip it up. *That's me gone!* you call out, one hand on the door frame, not moving. *I'm not here now!* Jennifer works nights and hasn't been to sleep yet. This is her midnight. She's in the bath, blowing at bubbles in her palm. *Sure you're not here*, she calls back, reaching for the bottle of white wine on the floor. *I can see that. Don't let the nasty men eat you up, okay?* She swigs and returns the bottle to the floor. *Remember, they can't prove anything.* A silence. Something occurs. *And if they can,* she says, *we'll just move to Arizona. I hate it here anyway.* Jennifer has this way of talking. You can't always trace the tone. *What?* you ask. *To where now? Where are we going?* You check the time. Maybe you should arrive early. *To Arizona!* she says. *We can put a pillow over Auntie Joan's head. No one will notice. Besides, she's like, a* **million** *years old. She* **wants** *to die. And then there's the land…* You understand, then smile. *I reckon I could be a farmer,* you tell her, stepping back into the hallway, still talking through walls. *You'd look good in dungarees. But what would we do with the body?* You look around at all the clothes on the floor, the half empty cans, the ashtrays, and think about staying at home today. Meanwhile, in the bathroom, Jennifer wiggles her toes, dips her head under the water and comes back up, a hat of white foam on her head. She says, *The body? Fuck it, I don't know, do I? We could bury her under the porch, or chop her up and feed her to the dog or something. We'll work it out! Daniel, we're supposed to be outlaws!* You can hardly hear her now. You're closing the door behind you. *I have to go,* you call out. *See you tonight. Or earlier.* Jennifer takes another sip of wine, picks the up phone off the side and calls her mother from the bath.

She wonders what really happened last week. You've told her already, but you have this way sometimes. She can't always trace the tone.

You walk down the old spiral staircase, tie tied tight, newly cleaned shirt smelling of detergent and still warm from a rare, brief clash with the iron. Your shoes are shined and buffed. The others in the office won't recognise you in a suit, but it doesn't matter. If you're gonna be saved, it's not smartness that'll do the saving. Right now, Greg is probably welcoming the guys from Head Office, the three of them planning their strategy over coffee, considering options. Or maybe Greg is showing them round the place, introducing them to a few of his office favourites, the ones he calls *my little stars*, by which he means *my little sellers*. Soon they'll all be sitting down in the boardroom, the three of them, using words like *protocol* and phrases like *you've got to make an example haven't you* while Andrea offers tea and old biscuits with a sigh. You can't think about that, or anything else. Why would anyone waste their time? Instead, you pick the iPod out of your pocket, and scroll the screen downwards as you walk.

It's a short journey to the office. Which is usually a good thing.

Around this time of year, deep in winter, when days are short, you have friends who have to shower and shave when it's still dark outside. Your brother works twelve hours at a time, eight till eight. The woman in the flat opposite leaves at six every morning, travelling for two hours before sunrise. That's ten hours in blackness every week, thinking while moving, and another ten on the return journey. Too much thinking leads to mistakes. Once, in the hallway, you told this neighbour about how you could almost see your desk from your bedroom window, like it was somehow a joke you could both share. She faked a smile while you told her about how you could put off getting up till half eight, sometimes quarter to nine, and *still* arrive early enough to make coffee before punch-the-clock time, slipping on your headset and making the first call of the day, all while still being basically asleep. Now you think of this, it doesn't seem like it was such a clever thing to say. She's a manager of some kind. Jennifer said she was off with depression for months. What's wrong with you? Why don't you think about other people? Perhaps the panel will ask that.

Some mornings, when you're tired or have a hangover, you calculate how much you save in travel costs every week by living so close to the office. Then you work out how much you save per year, and it makes you feel warmer. This morning is different though. This morning you dream of a lengthy commute. A long walk, a bus, a train across the city, maybe another walk. Enough time to wake up, think clearly, work out what the fuck you're gonna tell them. Just in case you decide to fight, or beg forgiveness. *Can I speak to the home owner please?*, you said, as you did a hundred times a day, as you'd been doing six shifts a week for months. *Are you aware you could save up to 50% on your energy bill by switching to a different provider?* Still, this short walk, down the hill, round the corner, across the main road and up the steps to the reception area – at least it's long enough to listen to one tune. As you step out onto the street, you realise you might not be making travel savings for much longer. Then you hit SHUFFLE, wondering what the machine will choose. The world is in your ears.

In the first few bars, you recognise it.

You don't usually believe in omens. But now you wonder.

This song always has the same effect. The first notes open a valve in your chest that releases all the pressures inside your body, a valve that usually you can't even find, never mind manipulate. It moulds you into a new shape. The shape of a taller, thinner man, who's standing upright. Or a smaller, fatter one reclining in a Jacuzzi, somewhere tropical. This morning the valve works fast and as the song builds you feel brighter, all that pressure seeping through your clothes and into the cold air around, spilling onto the pavement, the road. You breathe the pressure out, up, up, into the grey, away and over the tops of the tenements, thinking that maybe you were wrong. Maybe you can do this. The keyboards swell slightly, just slightly in your ears, that quick, faint arpeggio rising and falling, rising and falling, a sound almost too soft to be an instrument, and you briefly forget where you're heading to. Then you remember again, thinking to yourself: *I'd like to die please, in the next few minutes. And I'd like this song to be played at my funeral.* For a moment, this is your only wish, and you imagine mourners wondering what it all means as they listen. Why you've chosen this sound as your final statement. You quicken your walk to fall in time with the music. The clipped rim shot of wood on metal is your heartbeat. You consider good ways to go, and think of how Greg would cope with never getting to complete the disciplinary process. It's almost worth closing your eyes, breathing in and stepping into the traffic.

You reach the bottom of the road then turn the corner onto the main road.

You said, *Yes I know you already have a provider Mrs Pendleton, but what if I told you I could save you nearly seventy pounds?* On the other end of the line, she murmured, wanting to be polite, wanting you gone. She finally said: *How much?*

Thinking about Mrs Pendleton sets you thinking about writing a Will. It makes you want to spell out your instructions. Everything to Jennifer. Everyone else can go fuck themselves. Where are they this morning? Where is the calm, clear advice of friends and family? The support? Why does the phone not ring? As you think about this, you feel the beginnings of something like a prickly rising heat at the edges of your being, pulling you tight. It's a light fluttering in the rib cage. A sickly feeling in the stomach. What if you get run over before arriving at work? What if you die and they give you a funeral like your father's? You imagine some placid, bovine Servant of the Lord tweaking the speech he's been giving for decades, filling in the gaps where names need to be, talking about how really you were *a deeply spiritual person* who, though not a regular in the pews was an *upright and moral citizen* who *lived by Christian values*, and was now somewhere in the ether *being welcomed into God's eternal warm and loving embrace.* Thinking about God's eternal embrace, you feel your throat tighten, your breathing becoming restricted. You've got to be careful. You don't want to do anything which might end up killing you off before you've got the appropriate paperwork in order. Still, maybe it's worth living. There's always Arizona.

Something in you crackled, you thought of her standing there trying to get rid of you and you said, *Actually Mrs Pendleton, fuck it. Do you know what? Just fuck it. Fuck it all.* Mrs Pendleton didn't know what to say. Someone took the phone from her.

Even though nothing you need for this meeting can be found in your bag, you stop and check it again. Peering inside, you see that nothing has moved. What were you looking for in there? You think this thought as the first verse of the song comes to an end, volume rising, the buzz and hum of one guitar pouring into your left ear as the siren wail of the other screams in your right. You think of how no one else you know has even heard of this band, and in a way that makes them yours. They're from another planet. Canada. You've never seen them on television or heard them on the radio. You don't know what they look like. In your mind, they forgive all your sins. *Mrs Pendleton*, you said, before you started crying, not knowing it was no longer Mrs Pendleton you were speaking to, *Please Mrs Pendleton, just put the fucking phone down.*

The band plays in your ears, just for you.

They've been powering on, hitless, for a decade, singing songs about bitterness and bad credit and the power of rock 'n' roll. They're still playing clubs and fending off part-time jobs. They're still dreaming. This band says everything you want to say, better than you could ever say it.

The song swoops and dives and urges you on.

People walk past you in the other direction. Most are also listening to music through earphones, cocooned in their imaginations.

Some faces you recognise. You wonder if you look different to them this morning.

As you up your pace, getting closer, closer to that boardroom – why go at all? why not just run? – the song is into a chorus. It's pushing onward, onward, but it sounds exhausted, the singer's voice bruised and cracked, the sound of years of bedding down in cheap hotels and fans' bedroom floors, that sound bleeding through the little earphones into your head. He's telling you, this man who is more of a success than you'll ever be, but less than he wants to be, about how his soul wants to sing a hateful song, but he's refusing to do it. Even though it's in him to sing, aching to get out. You think to yourself: these sounds are made by people, by everything those people have ever done, seen, lost. Then you think: maybe when you die, you don't want a funeral at all. Maybe you'll throw a party instead. No solemn speeches, no mourning, no wringing of hands or regrets and no casket. Really, if you think about it, this is a positive, hopeful sound you're listening to. It's a survivor's song. And after all, you're a survivor. So if you *do* die today, your mourners could be dancers, their black hats and coats turned into floral pattern shirts and dresses, tears of sorrow transformed into tears of joy, each person reaching for the skies, singing along to your favourite song, theirs also, your brother telling a friend with a smile: *This is what Daniel would have wanted.* Then they'd go round in a circle and share their memories of you. Today, you're gonna survive. As you walk, you swell.

You imagine Jennifer scattering your ashes.

Then: your corpse being thrown out of a plane.

Then: ritual suicide at your desk.

Then: having a job you don't hate.

You cross the road at the lights, feeling strangely free, playing imaginary drums with your arms through the second chorus as you walk, not caring if anyone else sees, not caring what they think of you. Hitting the air feels like hitting Greg who will, by now, surely be aching for your arrival, the conversation with his superiors from Head Office now that bit more awkward, stilted, as the meeting approaches. The transcript of your crime will be typed and placed in front of each panel member, another copy typed by Andrea, for you, so you can't escape what you've said, every *fuck* circled and highlighted. Meanwhile, in the next room, rows of Greg's little stars try to forget what's happening to you as they pace through their lines, each call being recorded, while they search for that crucial next sale, pressing that bit too hard for a commitment so they can add another big tick to their sales figures and everyone can clap. Greg sometimes writes down things he wants to say in advance. He might have written down: *Do you know how much you scared Mrs Pendleton, Daniel? Do you think it's fun to take advantage of little old ladies? To attack the vulnerable in that way?* If he asks all that, and if you don't run out of the room or break into tears, you hope you'll have the courage to remind him that taking advantage of little old ladies is part of your fucking job description.

It's half way through the final chorus when you realise you might have misunderstood this piece of music. Competing with the growl and rev of noisy morning traffic, the words seem muffled, the distortion doesn't have the same crunch you remember, you think there's a lyric in there that you didn't notice before, you focus on it, the final line of chorus could mean just about anything, and in that split second all certainty evaporates. You wonder what this new uncertainty might mean. Then your mind is wandering again, and you wonder if maybe the song is not about love or hope but actually just about money, about how the men in this band never had any of it, and how really they don't know if they can go on like this much longer. Suddenly the song sounds like a kind of defeat. The drums sound tired, the thump of the bass tom sounds weak, like it's been punctured then taped up to cover the holes. The guitars sound old and battered, the leads appear to buzz. Vocals crackle into a smashed-in microphone. You imagine each band member trying to pretend they're somewhere else as they battle through this old tune one more time, maybe in front of a crowd of a thousand. Or twenty. Considering a career change. This song never used to sound like this. It must be you that's changed.

You turn the final corner.

I'm sorry Mrs Pendleton, you said, finally regaining your composure. *I'm sorry.*

You're probably just as well sticking with your current provider. Her son spoke quietly into the receiver. *You should be ashamed of yourself.*

Jennifer is right. What you need is not old words: what you need is Arizona. You picture your arrival at Arizona Airport (you don't know what it's called) picking up a convertible at Arizona Car Hire (or whatever) and heading out onto the Arizona freeway, top down, your hair blowing in the breeze with this song, this big noise blasting out of the speakers. (You have no idea about the landscape in Arizona, which other states it borders, whether it has call centres and bosses called Greg.) It's another universe you're in here, where this band are popular and rich and the song is on the radio all the time. Everyone knows the song, and it improves their lives, and it has improved yours, today, and will do every day from now on. Next to you, Jennifer is in big red sunglasses, holding a pillow in her left hand, wielding it like a hammer and saying, *It's what Auntie Joan really wants. And besides, what can she do with a hundred acres?* The two of you are laughing, kissing deep kisses, holding hands. You'll never see that old office again, or any office again. From here forward, each day will be a steady climb up a mountain which is satisfying but challenging, manageable, with no dips or unsteady passages, no loose rocks, consequences or unexpected bad news. Every year you will climb higher and one day you'll reach the top of the mountain and laugh about the time you were fired for crying and swearing down the phone to a stranger. *Do you remember those days?* you'll say to Jennifer, laughing. *Can you really believe that was us?* You won't hate Greg, though the hate is in you. You won't hate anyone at all.

As the last notes of the outro fade to nothing, you notice you've arrived at work. You switch the music off. It feels like hours since you left home. Standing outside the office block, looking upward, you hesitate, then check your bag one final time, for what you don't know. You can't remember whether you were supposed to bring anything along today. Then you text Jennifer. The message reads: ARIZONA? Then you step forward, buzz the office intercom, Andrea says, *Is that you, son?*, and you answer, *Dead man walking. Is the executioner here?*

Her laugh sounds like a cough.

She lets you up.

The reply comes through quickly, and you read it as you're climbing the stairs, headphones still in your ears.

It reads: REALLY?

David Wheatley

The President of Planet Earth

И с ужасом
Я понял, что я никем не видим,

Что нужно ссять очи,
Что должен сеятель очей идти!

And with horror
I understood – no one could see me.

I would have to sow eyes.
My task was to be a sower of eyes!

You were Xodasevich, I was Xlebnikov,
where the Cyrillic X marked the spot
and the Café Iskra rang with the forced laugh
of crewcut Futurists come to drink and plot.

That was the year Natalia fell for Boris,
who loved Anna, who loved Sergei in vain,
pince-nez'd, married Sergei she would embarrass
with harebrained sonnets trying to explain.

Chai-cup storms within a storming shark pool!,
where Acmeists would shout down party placemen,
Old Believers noisily talk bull,
and the silent ones were always secret policemen.

Do you remember our local Mayakovsky,
less a 'cloud in trousers' than a rain shower,
piddling revolution from on high
while we looked for an umbrella we could share?

Or our Esenin, signing with his blood
each update from his daily bust-up/love-in,
or bumptious, bourgeois Pnin who sat and blubbed,
poor man, how he had 'nofing left, nofing, nofing'?

But is that the fee-fi-fo-fum of the Kremlin
mountaineer approaching, scaling the onion
domes in Peter's Square? Your fear and trembling
at the age to come can never come too soon.

I still see the snow outside the Winter Palace
that January morning, splashed with sickening
raspberry ripple. The bloodlust never cloys,
but the blizzards of the lost will have their reckoning.

Hang more Professors!, Lenin telegrammed
drily to some Junior Dean of slaughter.
I've seen the dead dug up and altars grimed
with blood and shit by soldiers racked with laughter.

The show of red flags billowing in that heady
air like Isadora Duncan's scarf
choked as much as swaddled any Mayday
victory march declaring none would starve.

The emotions, it appears, are unskilled workers.
I never yet saw a quatrain stop a bullet,
but I've a fond delusion that recurs
a poet-king will one day top the ballot –

not any old poet, but Viktor Vladimirovich!
Otherwise swap a despot for a bard
and learn too late you're stuck with one of each,
and the execution warrant as high art.

Have you *seen* that rank Ossetian's doggerel,
targeting his words like a firing squad,
who couldn't find a rhyme for bugger all
and scans like a tank battalion on parade?

My favourite fruit is eyeballs, I still hear
my ravenous interrogator boast,
who kept his belly full and conscience clear,
my 'one-half Nero, one-half Jesus Christ'.

Still, inspiration, I wouldn't call you a gent
banging on the door at midnight, shining
a torch in my face like a Cheka agent,
you the sinned against and I the sinning,

crushing our offspring come the dawn like lice.
And yet they worship me and swarm back nightly
pleading filthily with me for their lives,
I, my poems' larval God-almighty!

I've also studied
    the staircase

        lineation
you use, Vlad,
    though seasick

       I confess,
or landsick
    at its all-out

       tumbling motion,
like the stop-go
    nude in Marcel

       Duchamp's canvas.

I'm a Rodchenko montage, Lily Brik-
meets-brontosaurus, beauty and the beast;
I'll bankrupt your aesthetics, go for broke,
a thundering slap in the face of public taste.

Calling down for room service I got
the year 1913 ('Is that the future?'),
and felt the time-lag give me it right in the gut,
knocked into next year like a prize fighter.

In an abstruse mathematical equation
I came upon the formula for war
in Japan and famine in the Volga Basin
and tried to pass my findings to the Tsar.

Take the circumference of a drop of blood
expressed as a ratio of the equator
and you've the secret, world-traversing code
that carries me from inner space to outer.

Alchemo-numerologically, nine
contains the answer to the *kulak* crisis.
The end to war's an undiscovered prime
of which, innumerates, we have but traces.

I who understand the language of birds
have risen up against the bully-boy sun,
hitched a lift on the comet-tails of words
and planted myself on his throne to pulse and shine.

Glossolalic pentecosts of trans-sense
(transmagnificanjewbangstantiality!)
putting to the sword the dragon one-sense
(zaumnostomniumhorrorshowreality!).

O tundra, steppe or taiga landscapes lacking
all horizon, face without a profile;
o winter sun these latitudes will blacken
until all-conquering seeds of light prevail!

Wandering the fly-blown road to Persia
I thought of you, Prometheus, on your rock,
served up for the tyrant gods' sick pleasure
in a soup of your own loins with liver stock

to that insatiable vulture Thou Shalt Not.
No guts need spill when I redeem mankind:
my brain's a honeycomb that all can eat
and live in too, a self-devouring hive mind.

Spying myself in a reservoir in Baku
I flinched from my Rasputin-like long hair.
Rublev's God, it's time that I forsook you;
your word of God's one cosmic-sized *longueur*.

The flame I light needs sacred mirth to fan it:
that's why I snort at *The Brothers Karamazov*.
The eternal silence of those infinite
spaces makes me want to laugh my ass off!

Ecky-thump way-I-tell-'em never-sunnier
tittyfalarious I-say-I-say tee-hee-hee!
Bitter/hollow/mirthless nothing-funnier-
than-unhappiness down-the-snout *smekhachi!*

All Russia is to me a living grammar
book and its map a verb I conjugate.
The dictionary I ride like a gray mare,
surveying my words like any head of state.

I dream of single-letter poems, each
an atom of the Slavic brain writ large –
my nano-epics *Kh, Sh, Ch* and *Shch*,
the diary of a trip to Prague called *Ř*.

Truly I am the president not just
of Russia but of Planet Earth, whose mission's
to transform the greatest and the least
of us from earthlings into pilgrim Martians.

Today you 'forgot to hang yourself', Kruchenykh.
I put a gun to my head and forgot to shoot.
My speed of thought's already supersonic.
I'll sew you a thinking cap from a winding sheet.

The skull to me was always a space helmet.
There's a planet named for me, 3112,
I yearn for like a melancholy soulmate;
I'll start the rocket, Russia, if you come too.

Revolutions eat poets, swallow them whole.
Somewhere in the Kremlin sewer there lurks
regurgitated, drowned and damned, the sole
surviving scrap of all my vanished works.

Isaac, you'll pioneer a whole new genre,
silence, but there's no dumb-show dumb enough,
no batting eyelid tics that don't spell 'goner'
in Morse code to your NKVD oaf.

And Isaac, not forgetting that tale of yours
I'm in where that blackguard takes my stallion –
my beauty bow-legged from some Cossack's arse –
while I end up deserting, weeping, wailing,

and over the noise of battle comes the motto,
louder than bombs, cannons and my curses,
'The whole world to us was as a meadow
in May crisscrossed by women and horses.'

Time the barber is Sweeney Todd-meets-Occam.
I speak with the clairvoyance of Armageddon:
Boris, beware a telephone call from Stockholm,
Osip, don't get on that train to Magadan.

Kruchenykh, you'll pant on to the Prague Spring –
Janáček erupting into doo-wop,
flower-power Communism – but not quite long
enough to look us up on Ubuweb.

Ah, internet! where all our dreams come true,
where Ron Silliman blogs for pure love
of the post-avant, and tweets and podcasts too,
and I am Facebook friends with Marjorie Perloff.

They like me will have had their share of ills
on the road to permanent Futurity –
tenure committees, Billy Collins' book-sales,
ripped-up tickets for that Swedish lottery.

Time is the breach that only time can mend,
the beating core of the caesium atom.
Eternity is to live in the present moment:
there and only there am I at home.

Byzantium's golden groves could not compete
with this desert of the real bleached to lead
where the hills ring to my Gul-Mullah's trumpet,
my white wings broken, my poor brain full of blood,

my poor brain wrecked on the reef of the world's 'No';
where I hurl my words at the sky to no avail,
buried under rockslides by their echo
snagged on my skull like a gramophone needle.

A child on the beach, I built my sand-castles
from the total grains of sand of human bliss
and skimmed rhymes out to sea, frail vessels
on trade routes far beyond all profit and loss.

Now otherworldly as you like a breeze
begins to trace the contours of my death mask,
my laments hurry me downhill like skis,
and life is a chewed and spat-out sunflower husk

That was the year Natalia fell for Sergei,
who loved… who had a fling with… who went mad…
But what are you doing, Russia, after the orgy
of history, if you're still in the mood?

You were Khodasevich, I was Khlebnikov;
am Khlebnikov, I am that vessel still
through whom all that was promised, broken off
mid-word, will yet arise in living steel.

Reviews

Dear World & Everyone In It: New Poetry in the UK Bloodaxe £12.00
Edited by Nathan Hamilton

Whatever we think of the top-end of po-biz these days, it is not running short of critics. The highly publicised tugs-of-war in the last few years, over the position of Oxford Professor of Poetry and over the editorship of *Poetry Review*, have given ample evidence of a scene which is unhealthily factionalised. Much of the criticism which is thrown around is noticeably harsh. Recently, reviewing Ed Dorn in the *London Review of Books*, Iain Sinclair, for example, complained of 'the movers and promoters of the established verse manufacturing orders, those sharky cultural bureaucrats and strategic prize-givers'. Similarly, Patrick McGuinness, guest-editing *Poetry Review* this year, describes a poetry culture which is 'consensus-stunned and stupefied with boosterism'.

What do you do, then, if you are a new poet who is arriving fresh to the party? How do you make your way in such murky waters? Nathan Hamilton's anthology *Dear World & Everyone In It*, which is a self-consciously youthful take on the current poetry culture, represents a partial but fascinating answer. The book's subtitle is 'New Poetry in the UK' and, for the purposes of inclusion, the (somewhat arbitrary) cut-off age is thirty-seven. Over sixty young (or youngish) poets have been included and the book's blurb announces an 'attempt to define a generation'. This claim is quite reasonable.

By virtue of having an enormous potential to influence poetry culture, anthologies are generally held to a special set of standards. They can succeed in two principal ways: (a) straightforwardly, as well-arranged collections of poems and (b) more rarely, as enduring cultural landmarks. One of my favourite anthologies, Patrick Crotty's *Modern Irish Poetry*, is a good example of the former type. It was not an *important* book – it did not redraw the literary landscape – but it was an excellent selection of poems, you could take it anywhere. If Hamilton's anthology succeeds at all, then it is in the second rarer way. It is not a particularly winning assortment of poems but it might be an important one.

I say that the anthology is not very good as a collection because the quality of its contents is distinctly mixed – amidst the finely executed poems there are some really awful ones. The way the editor introduces the book is also a problem and has drawn fire elsewhere. Because it is designed, to some degree, to draw attention to itself, the introduction is worth dwelling on for a while. In pursuit of liveliness, the editor allows himself an alarming degree of license and writes some very silly passages:

> Dear NASA, I saw today your Mars rover, Curiosity, landing. I would like to be a Mars Rover, parachuting onto other worlds, eating chocolate.

At times, Hamilton gives the impression that he wants not to introduce the poems, but to write about himself introducing the poems. More generally, the introduction tends to act as an extension of the poems themselves, being consistent in many ways with the cultural allegiances they display and with the stylistic procedures they follow. One of the persistent patterns of the poems, for example, is a reluctance to commit (to relationships, to political positions, to definitive statements) and the introduction is accordingly full of hedges and disclaimers:

> ...this is NOT an anthology of the *best young poets* in the UK.
> This is as good an anthology of good poetry written by as varied a group of poets and poetries as The Editor could have compiled currently and in the time given and for the money paid. That seems fair.

In not nailing his colours to the mast, Hamilton tends to dodge behind the thoughts of others, generously including suggestive quotations, reporting casual conversations, and engaging in comic asides. Another way in which he mildly imitates what he introduces is by adopting an (intermittently) epistolary style. Paragraphs affect to address various 'touchstone figures' ('Dear Simon Armitage...', 'Dear Luke Kennard...') as well as more humorous addressees ('Dear Jean Luc-Picard...', 'Dear Olympics...'). Reading through the book we find that several poems are, in whole or in part, also epistles including Ben Borek's 'Cisse Windsor Knot', Angus Sinclair's 'A Letter', and Steve Willey's 'Three Pages from *Signals*'. As a poetic form the letter goes in and out of favour – I would guess that its current popularity has something to do with our 'ever-messaging' culture. Certainly, the form fits in well with the book's pervasive chattiness and its evocation of closely-knit, knowing in-groups.

Despite the book's peculiar selection-policy, its daft introduction, and its magpie content-list, I do think that it should be taken seriously. It goes a long way to define a new generation of British and Irish poets and it also gives a sense of that generation's (considerable) force. There is a possibility – one wouldn't want to stress it more strongly than that – that, many decades hence,

Dear World & Everyone In It might be regarded as a major reference-point in the way that we look to such milestones as Geoffey Grigson's *New Verse* or Robert Conquest's *New Lines*.

One thing to which the anthology points is a cessation in the low-level conflict between British and American poetries – a cessation brought about by the complete victory of the latter (the anthology begins, pointedly enough, with an anecdote about watching a water-polo contest between the US and GB, which the US wins 'easily'.) This is a decisively American book, more specifically a book which is deeply indebted to the New York School. Dangerously easy to copy (but, as Michael Hofmann, once pointed out, hard to copy well) Frank O'Hara's coy and chatty style is everywhere – it is discernible, for example, on the first page of the introduction:

> Today, I want to be a water poloist. I imagine walking into the dive bar across Grand Street with my big pecs and, when someone asks me what I do, I say 'I play water polo', and instead of looking kind of surprised and sorry for me they look interested and look at my pecs.

Ashbery, too, has a walk-on part in the introduction. After that, Ben Stainton contributes a poem archly entitled 'Self-Portrait in a Concave Mirror', while Sam Riviere's 'Buffering 15%' begins, more or less explicitly, as a rewrite of 'The Day Lady Died':

> you aren't thinking clearly as you enter the bank
> on the day leslie nielsen dies
> the coldest december 'in living memory'
> mark's badge reads
> 'have a good time all the time'
> maybe you should think about getting a motto

So what has happened to cause the sharp change in poetic allegiances which we find in the anthology? There appear to be three principal factors: (a) the explosion of Creative Writing course in the past dozen years (b) the prevalence of social media (c) the economic crash. In reaction to an aging and corrupt poetry scene, all these features have encouraged a kind of stylistic extremism, with (b) and (c) doing much to amplify and sharpen the influences made available by (a).

While these tendencies have many positive results, one startling effect of reading the anthology is negative – realising the notes that the poems do not play. Certain long-dominant poetic styles appear to have been wholly eclipsed. One struggles to find a 'Sylvia Plath poem' for example – or a 'Ted Hughes poem', a 'Philip Larkin poem', a 'Seamus Heaney poem'. Meanwhile the daddy of them all – the 'Paul Muldoon poem' – which had seemed to bulldoze everything in its path (roughly in the period 1980–2000), has all but vanished.

Amidst this bonfire of the affinities, however, not all of the accustomed figures have been vaporised. Although it is not particularly obvious at first, the anthology is a tribute to Auden's continuing influence – *not* the Auden of *Another Time* (beloved of Larkin) but the very early Auden beloved of the New York School, author of the wildly extravagant 'Paid on Both Sides' and 'The Orators', as well as the more casual, informal author of poems like 'Tonight at Seven-Thirty' and 'The More Loving One'. Heavily represented by poets from the South-East of England, this is quite a London-oriented book, but it is London experienced as a kind of extension of New York (Ashbery's 'algorithm of other cities'), with the same kind of bright internationalism and liberal social attitudes – one thinks of Auden's later description of himself as a 'New Yorker'.

As opposed to what the book does not do, there is a remarkable consistency to the styles on view. What we find is not quite a family resemblance – it is more of a 'clan likeness'. It would take much more space than I have to go into this shared poetic landscape – it includes odd objects like knives and fridges, persistent techniques like repetition and ellipsis, a generous sprinkling of Internet-inspired typographical habits, an attachment to the prose-poem, an Audenesque sense of Us and Them, a profound anti-Romanticism and a deep suspicion of the vatic stance. Still, I will detail a few of the categories which I think are particularly relevant.

A steady theme of the poetry is the fear of transgressing some imperfectly understood contemporary law (a good subject for comedy). The poems are full of low-level misunderstandings, communications that don't quite hit their target. It is a poetry of semi-attachment.

> Anyway. We went for a drink and he ate and I didn't and at first we struggled with inevitable silences and when I spoke my voice sounded embarrassing with the possibility of tears…

(Emily Berry, 'The Way You do at the End of Plays')

The poets are, at once, hunted, sheltered (one might even say, *shy*), and short of cash. There is a general preoccupation with going to the bank and checking one's balance, and this goes along with a prevailing sense of reduced circumstances and diminishing returns (if any of these poets have a lot of money, they should probably keep quiet about it.)

The gods here are not savage – extremes of emotion are out. While there is little of Larkin in any of the poetry, what does survive of the Movement ethos is the sense that the poets and their speakers are experiencing life as gently miserable. Modern life, here, is rubbish – but only slightly so. The jokiness of the poems always feels like it flirts with a bearable form of depression ('this is me in public putting on a 2nd pair of sunglasses/because I feel suddenly like crying'.) Often the prevailing sadness is a subject for self-scrutiny, held out as in Jack Underwood's 'Sometimes your sadness is a yacht' as an object for dispassionate investigation:

> …today we hold it
> to the edge of our bed, shutting our eyes
>
> on another opened hour and listening
> to our neighbours' voices having the voices
> of their friends around for lunch.

In reaction to adverse circumstances, the best response appears to be humour of a slightly absurd variety. In a book where humour-failure is one of the greatest sins, the stand-up comedian becomes a kind of cultural hero. The introduction draws attention to this with several approving references to a particular comic routine – its final stand-alone sentence goes: 'Eddie Izzard in a dress saying BUnch of flowerrrrrs!' To some degree, this shows the cultural penetration of performance poetry – there are quite a number of (deflationary) punchlines. With their attachment to various types of repetition, poems in the anthology have a frequent air of 'the little routine', the party-trick, for which the audience is expectantly watching out.

In a manner strongly reminiscent of the New York School the poems often feature a peculiar colour field. Jonty Tiplady's 'Syndromes and a Century' begins, 'All the more ultramarine ailments/ disappear into a blue fox', while Amy De'ath's 'Vertigo Valley' begins, 'You arrived – it was unanticipatable, some bees even sang/ into a future cloud very far away and yellow.' In poems by different poets we encounter 'a scarlet day', 'raspberry jeans', 'violet arboretums'. Sam Riviere's speaker in 'Buffering 15%' thinks about, 'painting the fridge blue again', while a speaker in Katherine Kilalea's 'Hennecker's Ditch' prepares to eat 'a black lobster'. Bright, artificial colours are particularly favoured.

Despite the prevalence of odd colours, however, the 'house style' is not especially visual. More emphasis is placed on those senses which poetry can render better than television: touch and (especially) taste. Much of the surprise of the poems is dependent on the sudden appearance of unexpected flavours:

> In eye she gave me her
> crinkle of hair, clothed in
> aubergines.
>
> Cooked me, fed me horsemeat.

There is a steady connection made between food and wounding, often overlain with a kind of comic menace, as in Heather Phillipson's 'Although You Do Not Know Me, My Name Is Patricia':

> Some share life, like two unequal halves of a Chelsea Bun, with a stranger. Some release the sugared non-half into the mouth of a stranger. Some realise the unequal-half-fiddle once the sugar's all swallowed by a mouth that won't be around forever.

Not all of the poets fit in with the book's prevailing ethos but the vast majority do. Of course this has little effect on the successes and failures of individual poets. Sixty-plus poets is too many to include – about half of that number would have been advisable. Amongst the poets I especially enjoyed were Emily Berry, Luke Kennard, Emily Toder, Olli Hazzard, Katharine Kilalea, Jack Underwood, Patrick Coyle, Sam Riviere, Tim Cockburn and (my colleague) Sandeep Parmar. I also enjoyed poems by Frances Leviston, Sophie Robinson, James Byrne, and James Midgley.

This is not a book for readers coming to poetry for the first time. It is a book for people already on the inside of the scene. To the entirely uninitiated, I suspect the title will appear to announce a collection of poems by schoolchildren. Indeed, when (as a kind of test) I showed the book to someone with almost no knowledge of contemporary poetry this was her first surmise. Depressingly, after scanning the contents for some moments, she asked, 'did the poets pay to be included?' I include this observation in case anyone thinks that this is a populist book reaching – with evangelical fervour – beyond the usual poetry-reading public. It doesn't attempt anything like that. It is one of the anthology's main lessons: we are all coterie poets now.

John Redmond

Life After Life. Doubleday. ISBN 9780385618670. HBK. £18.99
Kate Atkinson

Her debut novel *Behind the Scenes at the Museum* (1995) may have won the Whitbread Award but these days Kate Atkinson is better known for her crime novels – like *Case Histories* (2004) and, most recently, *Started Early, Took My Dog* (2010) – featuring detective Jackson Brodie. This series has also been adapted for television by the BBC, set and filmed in Edinburgh – where Atkinson lives – even though most of the books are not. But anyone who's pigeon-holed her as a 'crime writer' will be soundly undermined by her stunning latest offering, *Life After Life*, which is a masterclass in 'what if' history and paean to the art of storytelling.

By constantly playing with time, *Life After Life* has the depth of a novel that spans generations, when actually it's simply reliving the same one endlessly. Ursula Todd is born on 11 February 1910 but dies a page later, strangled by her umbilical cord. In the next chapter, she lives, rescued by a doctor's surgical scissors. Ursula gets older and dies in a tragic accident. But a chapter later, she's beginning her life once again.

In this way, Ursula perpetually dies and is reincarnated as the same person, with the same family, and is given the chance to relive her life. The premise might sound contrived but Atkinson engages with it beautifully. Early on, Ursula is aware that something isn't quite right in her life, that some of her memories are from the future. Sometimes, this foresight doesn't save her; she knows the second – and the third, and the fourth – time round how to cheat death but it finds her anyway. But occasionally she pushes forwards, through the Great War and on to the next before the cycle begins again.

The novel opens in 1930, with Ursula attempting to kill Hitler – after all, she knows in her future-memory the devastation that he will cause. But it's the small ways in which she affects the pattern of ordinary lives that resonate most deeply. The chapters set during the Blitz are particularly mesmerising, alternating neatly between daytime banalities – the drudgery of office life, the necessary queues for bread – to night-time terrors: the vibrations of falling bombs, the soft squelch of a dead baby's body underfoot after a raid. These exquisitely rendered details make each of Ursula's lives seem more real than the last.

Her narrative often changes; in one life, for instance, she makes crushing mistakes in love that she avoids in the next. But some things stay the same. Her warm family and their idyllic suburban home, Fox Corner, always looms large. Her devotion to her father Hugh, her brothers Teddy and Jimmy, and her sister Pamela is constant; her indifference towards her mother Sylvie and older brother Maurice is too. These relationships are anchors in the perpetual retelling of Ursula's story, a soothing presence as the chaos of her many lives unfolds again and again.

Small, sensual images leap from the pages. As an infant with influenza in 1918, 'Ursula's lungs felt as if they were full of custard, she imagined it thick and yellow and sweet.' As a volunteer helping to recover bodies during the Blitz in 1940, she experiences 'the gruesome sensation of putting your hand on a man's chest and finding that your hand had somehow slipped *inside* that chest.' They're simply-told details but they make the experience of reading *Life After Life* almost tangible, effortlessly balancing its foundational magical conceit with textural realism.

By focusing on the pivotal moments that can change, and end, a life, the book is also a metaphor for the multiple possibilities of narrative. A linear plot would let Ursula lead only one of these lives: Atkinson instead chooses to let her live a seemingly infinite number, glancing on many genres in the process. Sometimes, Ursula's tale teeters on a murder mystery; at others, it's a domestic tragedy, a historical novel and occasionally a romance. This isn't indecision but homage, a salute to the unending potential of storytelling across the ages.

Indeed, literature is one of the constants in Ursula's many lives. Fox Corner, her family home, has more than a touch of *Howards End* in its stable, English roots and quotes from great literature pepper her every incarnation. In her early life, the wisdom of Austen is quoted; in the darkness of the Blitz, Marvell's 'To His Coy Mistress' seems strangely appropriate.

These allusions remind us how comforting poetry and books can be in trying times and this blissfully moving novel is no exception. In constantly regifting life to Ursula, Atkinson makes the tragedy of death all the more heartbreaking. With gut-wrenching realism, she subtly reminds us that the book's central idea is a fantasy: that no matter how many 'what if' moments we may have, life happens only once. *Life After Life* is a dazzling achievement that compels you to return to the start once the last page has turned, to continue the cycle of Ursula's story and contemplate the limitless possibilities of existence.

Yasmin Sulaiman

Omnesia. Bloodaxe. £9.95 x 2, 172pp + 175pp.
W.N. Herbert

There is a Tom Waits story about a judge in Tennessee telling a defendant he knows he's guilty but letting him go anyway, since he couldn't possibly send an innocent man to prison. How does that work, you may ask yourself. In the same way that poetry readers can now amuse themselves swapping stories of how they love W.N. Herbert's *Omnesia* – altogether a better book than that other one of his, what's it called, *Omnesia*. The Tennessee judge was addressing a pair of conjoined twins, in case you haven't worked it out. We can address ourselves to *Omnesia* the 'remix' or *Omnesia* the 'alternative text'. As to which is the original version, I presume the answer is both. Or neither.

It may be just a personal thing, but I find it difficult to contemplate the covers of *Omnesia* and their flying cephalopod without thinking of Captain Beefheart's 'A squid eating dough in a polyethylene bag is fast and bulbous. Got me?' Herbert is the Captain Beefheart of Scottish poetry, makin ane almichty reerie-rairie o' a blether to himself, in his Scots poems at least, which may seem like orchestrated chaos at first but whose musicality and meaning reveal themselves little by little until it all makes sense. Well, most of it.

Omnesia embodies the condition of knowing everything and having forgotten it all too. '*You'd like to think it's God that sees ya*', Herbert writes in his title poem, '*and not the eye of Blind Omnesia*', which reminded me of an old argument about the existence of God. Is there anything an omnipotent God can't do? No. Then God must also not exist, since otherwise he fails the test of not being there. Consider Herbert's thoughts in Jerusalem's Church of the Holy Sepulchre:

> Because belief could choke this well,
> the world was emptied to a shell
> where places like Byzantium fell
> because what was not here was Hell.
> We queue to touch an emptiness
> that means our suffering must be blessed.

Omnesia is strung together from sequences describing jaunts (is there a 'jauntier' poet than Herbert?) to China, Venezuela, Russia, Israel, Somaliland and other parts, with the British Council picking up at least some of the bills, I hope. Bearings are easily lost. The Somaliland sequence is (partially) reproduced in both books, and seems key to the whole enterprise. Herbert also returns to the same poem 'Pilgrim Street' throughout both collections, or the same poem in instalments rather, almost symmetrically and consistently but not quite. Yet each section of the poem is different depending on its neighbour poems, just as a story told in heaven is different from the same story told in hell, as one of Herbert's epigraphs insists.

In the absence of a more detailed critique, how to give even a flavour of this unclassifiable book? There is something straightforwardly preposterous about Herbert's polyglot tendencies, ability to hoover up foreign cultures, and air of keeping the *Princeton Encyclopaedia of Poetry and Poetics* open on his desk at all times. So preposterous, in fact, that I suspect Herbert shares with the late Jocky Wilson a profound agoraphobia and never ventures outside his front door. At this point we might point to Herbert's use of Scots as a way of tying up the parish and the globe. There can be few things worse in the poetry world than the fake internationalism Herbert has satirised in 'Petrovich's Handy Phrases for the Visiting Writer':

> Thank you are for greeting me my brother/sister.
> You are a great poet. I have never
> heard of you before this moment.

Yet somehow Herbert's internationalism incorporates and subsumes all the fakery, just as his use of Scots ('a language filled with forty synonyms for snot') *could* be a Dundonian muttering in a bar, but in reality is among the most sophisticated of the many registers on which these poems draw.

There remains the question of scale. This is one short book review but these are roughly six slim volumes' worth of poetry, by conventional standards. Is it all too much to absorb? By way of a roundabout answer, I would suggest that what Herbert is up to with his maximalism is trying to heal the breach between the early MacDiarmid of the Scots lyrics and the wordy but predominantly Scots-free later epics. Some of the funniest moments here occur in the parodies of MacDiarmid in 'A Myth of Scotland':

> Ae dreich forenoon whaur the spew's whummelt
> Eh heard thon gantin soon
> a gutterjaw wi'iz harns kicked oot
> address the mune.

This is not just a tension in MacDiarmid's work but in his legacy too, with precious few contemporary Scottish poets looking to take up where the MacDiarmid of *In Memoriam James Joyce* left off. Frank Kuppner is a partial exception (his *Arioflotga* has many Herbertian affinities), but Kuppner has shown little interest in writing in Scots. I am not suggesting Herbert has taken it upon himself to perform a one-man rescue mission, but what he does provide in large amounts is a rambunctious humour, scholarly and slapstick – humour that is a lubricant that for any number of awkward conversational silences in Scottish literary history. For this I salute him, with extravagant admiration and envy. *Omnesia* is a wonderful achievement.

This review too is available in dual-format, with my other text appearing simultaneously in the *Dundee Courier* and giving him a much harder time than I've done here, can I just say in conclusion.

David Wheatley

The Sun King. Gallery Press. ISBN 978 1 85235 547 0. PBK. €11.95
Conor O'Callaghan

> *Time and again, we found a place that is as difficult to pin down and define*
> *as poetry, but like poetry, you'd know it when you saw it. It often contained*
> *decay and stasis, but could also be dynamic and deeply mysterious. Edgelands*
> *are always on the move.*
>
> Paul Farley and Michael Symmons Roberts (*Edgelands*)

Conor O'Callaghan is the laureate of the edgelands, those haunted, detritus-strewn liminal spaces on the borders of communities. From the beginning of his publishing history with Gallery Press, O'Callaghan has scavenged this terrain, exploiting its imagery in his quest for an aesthetic that reflects both his appreciation of poetic traditions but also his need to clear and develop new spaces. Gone is the mythologised bog-and-swan approach to composition; the too-readily deployed shorthand of the stock Irish lyric that comes preloaded with a sentimental and often conservative agenda. As he writes in 'The Peacock', from his third collection, *Fiction* (2005), a new wave of Irish poets has 'perfected that disappearing trick. / I'm thinking especially of that old lie / called sentiment and sentiment's rhetoric / that we, together or alone, no longer buy.' O'Callaghan is the forerunner of a generation of poets that includes his champions David Wheatley and Justin Quinn and a younger set that includes the likes of Leontia Flynn, Alan Gillis, and Matt Kirkham – all of whom look to reinvigorate a poetic practice in danger of riding the coat-tails of its internationally fêted sons and daughters.

In O'Callaghan's first collection, *The History of Rain* (1993) the poem 'Landscape' opens with a rejection of the customary 'Oirish' pastoral:

> It's a view that seems all too familiar.
> From where a gate fades into the foreground
> a whole landscape stretches away between
> what is already known and what is seen,
> to where the earth rinses into the sky
> and a town glimmers in another age.

We are in the edgelands 'between' the rural and urban, 'between' contemporary reality of what 'is seen' and the sentimenatlised glimmering town of a bygone era. If memory serves, there are sixty-eight instances of the word 'between' in O'Callaghan's first three collections. We are continually placed 'between' the town and the country, sea and land, the past and the present, interiors and exteriors, America and Ireland/England; or we are travelling above and through landscapes in planes or cars. These landscapes are littered with waste of liminal spaces– antiquated machinery, Coke cans, betting slips, dog shit, and the like. His fourth collection from Gallery Press, *The Sun King,* continues in this vein, exploiting personal and physical edgelands for poetic gain.

The collection's opening poem, 'Lordship', picks up where 'This', the last poem in *Fiction,* left off. In that closing poem O'Callaghan typically deconstructs the writing process, positing various scenarios in which 'something' (he's fond of an indefinite noun) gave rise to the finished product, before offering a truth, of sorts. In 'Lordship', the compositional games continue, opening with an image of a writer behind glass doors, as if on display, *not* writing what he initially intended. Glass- and screen-doors, car windscreens, and gaps in hedges are images that repeat throughout the collection, divisions between worlds that afford a blurring of boundaries. 'Lordship' goes on to blur borders between first, second and third pronouns and, as with 'Landscape', there is a transition between two eras that leads to a reinterpretation of the view. We arrive at a point in a poem about illicit sexual encounters, where a personal and literary fiction is created in which 'The truth, much as time does, vanishes behind' (l.47) and we are placed in the liminal, derelict edgelands, this time in ghost estates:

> I ran low on juice on the dual carriageway south
> that narrowed to a dirt track dead-ending at aftergrass
> where the house no longer stood
>
> and the bay had retreated into its shell of cloud
> and real estate signs were popping along the coast
> like crocus bulbs come late to flowering.

Those familiar with O'Callaghan's work will read in these lines echoes of older poems, such as 'Seatown', 'East', 'The Gate Lodge' and 'Landscape with Canal'. Indeed, each poem (each collection) should be read as part of a larger whole that, together, expresses O'Callaghan's aesthetic goals and preoccupations. In *The Sun King*, in addition to the exploitation of border territories, he continues to exploit the lexis of computer technology (see 'The Server Room', in particular), he reinvigorates fixed expressions and idioms, he plays with form, and he isolates the narrator within landscapes. It is this isolation and playfulness that are particularly to the fore in *The Sun King* and these aspects of the work are among the collection's great strengths.

While O'Callaghan is regularly a jack-the-lad, unreliable narrator he can also be brutally honest about personal circumstances and this fourth collection is his most intimate to date, haunted by the deterioration of a long-term relationship. It is perhaps insolent to suggest this circumstance generates greater lyrical beauty, but there are poems here that are searing in terms of their restrained pathos. The narrative voice is remote throughout the collection: alone with, and obsessed by, a salvaged wood-burning stove ('Woodsmoke'); at home while the family shops ('Among Other Things'); driving alone 'between school and here' ('Swell'); observing the aging and long-absent father asleep ('Mid to Upper Seventies'), and so on. And everywhere there are the signs of lives abandoned: 'farmyard instruments / scattered like punctuation marks' ('Translation'); 'real estates / pre being repossessed by ghosts' ('Tiger Redux'), 'a crossword left unfinished on a stoop' ('In Praise of Sprinklers').

One of the collection's strongest poems, 'Kingdom Come', is a lamentation dedicated to the poet Vona Groarke, in which the narrator parks outside the house the couple once shared, observing the old neighbourhood. All the O'Callaghan hallmarks are present. We are in the suburban edgelands where lawns serve as boundaries. Computer imagery is present in 'a screensaver reflected in the screendoor.' And there is the ubiquitous detritus of our lives: 'neighbours wheel their trash / to the sidewalk', and a chandelier prism refracts light across yards in which 'each lost wish still chimes'. But it is precisely this detritus, these scraps of our lives, that the narrator values and begs to recover when he prays:

> […] whatever kingdom come there is
>
> is a street we owned a place on
> where the life we meant to love
>
> and ran screaming from mid-stream
> completes itself without us

As is typical of O'Callaghan, the playfulness of his writing serves as a rejoinder and counterpoint to any charge of sentimentality. With an adherence to Yeats's 'singing line', there is a Muldoon-like *joie de vivre*, epitomised in 'Tiger Redux', which employs Blake's tyger (complete with pounding tetrameter and rhymes) to comment on boom-and-bust economies. The sonnet, 'The End of the Line', is printed sideways on the page in order to extend and delay the end of that line. Also printed sideways is the long final poem, 'The Pearl Works', a sequence of forty-five couplets, each precisely 140-characters long, that first appeared on a Twitter page. The sequence takes its name from a disused cutlery factory in Sheffield (a quintessential edgelands structure) and as personal circumstances change over the course of one year the narrator looks out across a neighbourhood reinvigorated by Chinese restaurants. If certain poems in the collection are reflective, here in this evolving landscape, even the May wind urges change: 'refresh, refresh, refresh'. As if in response, the poem builds a rich tapestry of sounds until it explodes into an assonant orgy of O's, closing the collection with a commemoration of the glories that 'Life' (and poetry) can afford:

O heliotrope O blosson bole O trompe l'oeil orange grove we home in
O old soul, no bones glowworm with whose strobe we's mope eternal gloaming

O closing words O lovely hopeless song (one more!) invoking love gone south
O storeroom door that's on a slope & opens outwards O open mouth

Miriam Gamble, writing of a new generation of Irish poets (and herself part of that generation) suggests '[their] poems occupy indeterminate zones, mediating between redundant pasts and nebulous futures, questioning the rhetoric of progress even as they seek adequate modes of resolution.' That's an effective summation of O'Callaghan's entire oeuvre. Few writers exploit the metaphoric potential of detritus quite as he does, and his sustained recycling process makes him a preeminent (if yet unacknowledged) eco-poet. O'Callaghan should be recognised more readily as the poet who has guided us systematically through the edgelands, and that he has done so with great acuity and poetic skill.

Paul Maddern

Burnt Island. Salt Publishing, ISBN 9781907773488. PBK. £8.99
Alice Thompson

Muted colours shadow the stark image of a solitary figure on the cover art of *Burnt Island*, Alice Thompson's sixth novel. Like the juxtaposition of light and dark in Salvador Dali's painting, Thompson invokes surrealist extremes in the literary and psychological framing of this narrative, which begins and ends with visual contrasts of black and white, providing a focal point of terror. While themes such as isolation and the quest for knowledge are reminiscent of her earlier fiction, *Burnt Island* reflects a shift in Thompson's writing.

Previously Thompson's experimentations with form and genre have inspired her to pay homage in her writing to authors such as the Marquis de Sade, Robert Louis Stevenson and Ian Rankin. *Burnt Island*, however, delves into the genre of horror fiction, like John Burnside's *Glister* or Louise Welsh's *Naming the Bones*. Thompson retreats from the urban locale of her Portobello-based novel *The Existential Detective* (2010) to the sphere of an island; however, unlike *Pharos: A Ghost Story* (2002), this is not a 'Scottish' novel with a nationalistic agenda or historical setting. *Burnt Island* is concerned with the primary theme of the horror genre – fear. In setting this horror novel on an island, Thompson uses a finite geographical space to expose an individual's core fears and a family's secretive dynamic, thus offering an infinitely complicated story that taunts assumed ethical and artistic boundaries.

Thompson introduces a male protagonist, Max Long. A mid-career author, Max desires public acclaim, literary plaudits and sexual liberation. Offered a writing fellowship at James Fairfax's home on Burnt Island, Max is determined to write a bestseller, but instead he wrestles with his own writer's block, the inevitable demise of his family and the overtures of the island's women – one of whom is his benefactor's daughter. The taboos of incest and murder are entwined with the taboo of authorial theft when Max's sponsor and rival trespasses these boundaries in both his personal and professional life. As the narrative fragments into a dream-like sequence, Max's longing for creative and sexual release ultimately outstrips his attempt to control his physical behaviour and psychological state.

Although the novel's twenty-four chapters are framed within a somewhat unnecessary Prologue and Epilogue intended to provide resolution to the disintegrating plot, these also serve to redirect the focus to the threat of plagiarism that is spun throughout the story. Since Thompson has admitted that 'each time with my next book, I think – "right, I'm going to make this popular", and each time, I just end up writing the book I had to write', it may be tempting to assume that Max Long is simply an extension of herself. Does Thompson simply plagiarise her own life as a writer? Retreating to a pseudo-autobiographical reading may, however, place artificial limitations on the narrative's detailed intricacy.

This is a book about writing; the brilliance of the novel lies in its narrative style. Initially, the prose seems self-conscious, cumbersome. To a reader familiar with literary tropes, the overabundance of similes and metaphors that populate the beginning pages use thematic clichés to parody Max's literary mediocrity. The writing – and the reading – of the narrative's beginning are laborious. Mimicking Max's writer's block, the first several chapters appear to rely on formulaic strategies to develop the plot; however, this tactic soon exposes Thompson's dexterity at her craft.

As the plot becomes increasingly fragmented and unhinged, Thompson's writing transgresses the generic confines of realist, Gothic and horror fiction. Her writing renders intermittent alterations of time and place, disrupting the reader's preconceptions of stability, while simultaneously invoking the reader's psychological fears and causing physical agitation. Non-sequiturs between considerations of life, art, and language; horror of doppelgangers and betrayal; and humorous anecdotes of the writing process reveal Thompson's flexibility within generic formulae. Transcending into surrealistic, yet articulate descriptions, the narrative unites the possessed soul of a maniacal writer and the sinister fear of plagiarism with the serene setting of sea and snow. Thompson's writing offers wisps of detail that allow the reader to revel in sensory impressions and psychological illusions. *Burnt Island* is a lyrical novel that offers delight not only for readers who seek a comfortable formula, but also for those who relish the freedom to enter an unstable and uncanny space of light and dark, horror and beauty.

Linda Tym

Where Rockets Burn Through: Contemporary Science Fiction Poetry From the UK.
Penned in the Margins. ISBN 9781908058058. PBK. £9.99
Edited by Russell Jones; Preface by Alasdair Gray

Is all poetry thought experiment? It can certainly widen our sense of what's possible. Considered in these terms, poetry and science fiction seem like a natural combination. But what is science fiction poetry? In his preface to this anthology Alasdair Gray makes the case that both Dante's *Divine Comedy* and Milton's *Paradise Lost* are science fiction poems since they describe 'wonderfully strange lives as if they were possible'. Editor Russell Jones addresses the question in his introduction but notes that any description of the genre is contentious, adding that he simply asked contributors to 'write something which speculates about alternatives, with a scientific edge'. As someone narrow-minded enough not to be automatically turned on by the prospect of poems about aliens and ray guns, I was happy to have my preconceptions about science fiction poetry zapped by Jones's broad remit.

The anthology is divided into four themed sections, each launched with a poem by Edwin Morgan, to whose memory this collection is offered in tribute, his work having inspired the science fiction poetry of many writers. There are contributions from over forty contemporary poets living in the United Kingdom, including American, Australian and Danish writers. As well as newer names there are established poets such as Brian McCabe, Ron Butlin, Jane McKie, Dilys Rose and W.N. Herbert – this list indicating the Scottish slant to the anthology. There are also writers who are prominent in the world of science fiction writing including Jane Yolen and Steve Sneyd, the latter providing an introductory essay, pleasingly titled 'Wormholing into Elsewhere'.

The poems here emphasise both 'science' and 'fiction', which is to say that some are concerned with current science and its impact on our lives, and some are fantastical engagements with science and the possible futures of mankind. At almost 200 pages this is an eclectic and generous book with scope for various forms and styles including free verse, lyric, narrative and concrete poems, as well as diverse subject matter – while space travel, robots and aliens do feature, there are also poems about photography, genetics and climate change. Although science fiction seems to lend itself to apocalyptic and dystopian scenarios, there is much humour here, for example in James Robertson's combination of Scots with solipsistic perceptions of reality, 'Wha's jist a thochtie in anither's heid?', and his rendering of space dust as 'astral stour'.

Romance is a persistent topic too: Joe Dunthorne's poem 'Future Dating' depicts speed dating with automatons, and in 'The Costume' Aiko Harman tells of a Halloween robot costume that becomes permanent, inspiring a 'cool, metallic love.' In a touching lyric poem, 'The Trekker's Wife', Claire Askew adds an erotic dimension to the famous *Star Trek* phrase:

> He handles me gently,
> a microscope, an airlock door,
> the Universe – he goes boldly
> where no man has gone before.

A recurring (although usually implicit) question in this anthology is what makes us human. In 'The Last Human' Kona Macphee imagines a genetically modified race of humans that is immortal, musing that once such a step had been taken it would be irreversible:

> for who could look
> their own child in the eye, and tell her that
> among her classmates she would age,
> would die, and by a willed abstention?

A more flippant take on the topic of identity is Ross Sutherland's 'The Circus' in which he insists, 'It was difficult to remember what my penis looked like / amongst all those fake memory implants', which made me laugh out loud until I remembered that some people probably can't remember what their body looked like before their 'fake… implants'. The posthuman world is already with us.

There are a number of longer pieces, such as Matthew Francis's wonderfully whimsical tale of a man transported to the moon by a flock of geese. He looks back on the earth which is 'smudged with forests, doodled with coastlines' and asks 'How had I lived there?' Human beings are curious creatures, poets no less than astronauts or quantum physicists. There are no limits to our wondering about what Jane McKie calls, 'the subtle / radiant dark' and the poems here are testament to both our curiosity and our fears. The final word is given to Edwin Morgan's 'Riddle' – I won't give the answer away but it draws attention to a quality shared by both poetry and science. The anthology as a whole echoes many of Morgan's own concerns and themes and is a fine tribute to him.

Vicky MacKenzie

Republics of the Mind: New and Selected Stories. Black and White Publishing. ISBN 9781845024918. £9.99
James Robertson

Robertson's fifth novel, *The Professor of Truth,* is being published as this is written. In that text he re-examines the Lockerbie bombing in fictionalised form. He has publicly declared that Scotland must deal with this perceived miscarriage of justice as part of the process of freeing itself both politically and culturally. This collection of short stories, his third, is also concerned with that process: in the period since the earliest eleven stories (which appeared in *The Ragged Man's Complaint,* 1993) Scotland has gained a parliament and is now building up to a referendum on independence. The collection also offers an opportunity to compare the author's work some seven years before his first novel was published with work completed during the period in which he has become an established, award-winning author.

That great exponent of the short story, V.S. Pritchett, stated that a writer lives 'on the other side of a frontier'. This Bakhtinian notion of the necessity of otherness and difference as a creative force is at the heart of much of Robertson's work and this collection reflects that. The new stories present and challenge perspectives across a number of different 'frontiers': from that between fate and free will ('The Shelf') to the cartographic line ('The Dayshift'), to the moral ('Opportunities'), the physical ('Willie Masson's Miracle', 'The Rock Cake Incident'), the cultural ('Don't Start Me Talkin''), the rational ('The Dictionary', 'Old Mortality') and sometimes multiple combinations of these ('MacTaggart's Shed', 'The Future According to Luke', 'Sixes and Sevens'). These last three stories appear to be the most recent and are in many ways the most interesting.

The theme of 'MacTaggart's Shed' sits alongside that of his current novel: how does one move on from an atrocity? In the story, Robertson imagines the horror of 'ethnic cleansing' in a version of modern Scotland. The mundane Scottishness of the title is matched by the local and personal nature of the violence. The characters occupy a recognisably Scottish milieu, whilst storing caches of weapons and living amongst the burnt-out remnants of their neighbours' houses. It is an unsettling vision, and persuasive of the dangers of any crude nationalism.

Robertson's refusal to privilege a normative, rational point from which to view the irrational elements of the human experience leaves his vision of modern Scotland insistently unstable; a country full of possibilities rather one locked into the conflicts of the past. 'The Future According to Luke' tells of a night's drinking by three young Lakota men. Luke Stands Alone insists he has visions of the future but most of them are of events that have already happened and both the serious themes and humour of the story derive from this: 'They both liked drinking with Luke, even if he was a shit prophet, because he didn't want to fight either.' The relative familiarity of the scenario combined with the matter of fact acceptance of the notion of prophecy joins many of Robertson's stories and novels in challenging the 'otherness' of the 'other'. The complexity of the relationship between history and the present is also highlighted here, as it is in the final story ('Sixes and Sevens') where a visitor to former hospital buildings appears to slide from a rational present to confinement in irrational confusion, which leads one to question the 'reality' of the opening perspective.

Hogg's influence is also present in a number of the earlier stories, such as 'Tilt' and 'Bastards'. In the later tales, the potential absurdity of seeking certainties is highlighted when a woman enters a music shop hoping to be told what sort of music she likes ('Don't Start Me Talkin'(I'll Tell Everything I Know)'). Curiously, Hogg's influence is particularly notable in 'Old Mortality', which sardonically engages with the historical character who so fascinated Walter Scott. Robertson's story muses on Scottish culture, love and the fleeting permanence of humanity in its interaction with the landscape. It also contains one of the most evocative images in the collection: 'Through an iron kissing-gate was the roofless church, surrounded by old gravestones and tablets set at odd angles like wreckage bobbing in a green sea.'

'Republic of the Mind' is one of the original eleven stories. The central character, Robert, has retreated from the frustrating political reality of modern Scotland to a happier Platonic republic. There are many characters struggling with the 'frontier' between imagination and external realities in both halves of the collection. Robertson implies that this issue is particularly pertinent to the current Scottish situation, hooking the collection into the 'stateless nation/nationless state' discourse). In fact, if the collection has a weakness, it is that the stories too often seem to push the reader towards allegorical political readings. On the other hand, that might just be the weakness of the present reader, or the increasing urgency of the changing political context in which these stories must now be read.

'The Dayshift' depicts a bewildered old border guard in an unidentified nation where a tyranny has been removed.

Most of the people at the border did not even have their papers with them. Their *identity* papers. They had deliberately left them behind, or decided not to reveal them. That was what they wanted to be – anonymous. He found that hard to fathom. Why would anyone want to be anonymous? They claimed they wanted to be individuals but how could you be without your identity?

Here a really interesting premise is very effective in highlighting the personal dilemmas and confusions when exchanging the 'reassuring' certainties of tyranny for the yawning chasm of freedom. The station masters in the unnamed state stand to attention as the train goes by; 'as if they did not know how else to stand in a world that was no longer real.'

In this collection, the final frontier worth mentioning – other than space – is ecological: that between humanity and the non-human 'other'. The bobbing seal's head in *And the Land Lay Still* also haunts the earlier 'Republic of the Mind'. The opening story, 'Giraffe' sets up a number of thoughtful parallels between the human and animal inhabitants of a Highland safari park. At times it seems that those parallels, too, are intended to extend to the present situation of Scotland, via the nexus of social and environmental justice.

The reissued stories certainly gain increasing resonance in the current context. The collection overall offers a thoughtful and at times warmly amusing series of tales. They ask the sorts of questions which will become increasingly urgent in the coming months and years. The answers may well elude us, as they do many of the characters in the stories, but the themes which resonate throughout suggest Robertson's exciting sense of the cultural and political possibilities of the present moment.

Martin Philip

Nice Weather. Farrar, Strauss and Giroux. ISBN 978 0 374 22194 2. HBK. $24
Frederick Seidel

'The mother of the woman I currently/ Like to spank, I'm not kidding,/ Was my girlfriend at Harvard […] Please don't tell me/ Anyone reading this/ Believes what I'm saying or doesn't, it's irrelevant' ('School Days: III *Pretending to Translate Sappho*'). This is how Frederick Seidel has developed his confessional mode: by drawing our attention to the artifice of it. *Nice Weather* is his eleventh book of poetry and is stylistically linked to the late period of *Evening Man* (2008) *Ooga-Booga* (2006), and *The Cosmos Trilogy* (2003 – a massively underrated work loosely based on Dante's *Divine Comedy*, inspired by quantum mechanics, the new Hayden Planetarium, and New York). Alongside short lyrics and longer, looser pieces, the tone of *Nice Weather* is more consistently elegiac, concerned with a lifetime of memories and poems dedicated to dead college friends as well as literary figures.

By the end of 'Dawn', the first poem in *Nice Weather*, a tired, English appropriation of an Homeric epithet is subverted: 'The prostitute – whose name is Dawn –/ takes the man in her mouth and spits out blood,/ Rosy-fingered Dawn'. The semantic field crosses over from puerile 'waking up in the crack of…' territory, into *new* weather. The horror of this early morning fellatio is not the first time a Seidel poem has provoked a physical reaction in me when reading, and that is the point: Seidel is giving something to reader that was not previously there, recalling Ezra Pound's gloss on *Hamlet*: 'When Shakespeare talks of the "Dawn in russet mantle clad" he presents something which the painter does not present. There is in this line of his nothing that one can call description; he presents'. Pound's own take on the dawn of *Hamlet* is interesting here, since Seidel's famous visit to Pound in hospital is in itself an event worthy of the political complication, private pain, and taboo of a Seidel poem: Seidel, the young Jewish poet, visited Pound, the anti-Semite, in order to learn from him. The shade of Pound is also in 'Arnaut Daniel':

> Ezra Pound channeling the great troubadour poet Arnaut Daniel
> In St. Elizabeth's Hospital for the criminally insane
> In Washington, D.C.,
> Thanksgiving weekend, 1953,
> I remember sounded like he
> Was warbling words of birdsong.

Seidel's approach to death and elegy is crystallised in 'Cimetière du Montparnasse, 12ème Division', where a visit to the graves of Samuel Beckett and Susan Sontag is brought to a gruff conclusion: 'And now it's time to get the fuck out/ Of this beautiful pointlessness'.

Stunning opening lines abound, 'I impersonate myself and here I am,/ Prick pointing to the moon, teeth sunk into your calf' ('Rome'), and the endings of Seidel's poems are frequently unexpected, dazzling, and troubling. At the start of 'Then All the Empty Shall be Full, 'The shorebirds and the shellfish make merry in the giant oil spill', but the ending leaves ambiguous possibilities: 'I grab the supertanker by a hawser and I pull,/ And rewrite everything I ever wrote'. This conceit marries environmental disaster with literary destruction. Seidel takes everything personally. Either this is an environmental clean-up, and the creation of new poems, or the supertanker is merely dragging more oil through the sea, making every white page of Seidel's poetry black. Seidel also takes a retrospective look at his work to date, in a poem named after his lime-black-and-red-covered *Poems 1959–2009*:

> You know the poems. It's an experience.
> The way Shylock is a Shakespearience.
> A Jew found frozen on the mountain at the howling summit,
> Immortally preserved singing to the dying planet from it.

Updating Whitman's 'barbaric yawp', the sound of Seidel's 'Ooga-Booga' howls out across American poetry.

Seidelian metaphor is a method through which the Self can metamorphose at will through unexpected pathetic fallacy, or open out meaning through conceit. In 'Victory Parade', sex and contemporary politics are blended, where a girlfriend's 'new bikini trim,/ A waxed to neatness center strip of quim' is juxtaposed with 'the other drastic act/ Of display today – Osama bin Laden is dead!' The contemporary paranoia among many English poets, that treats with suspicion any poem that steps outside safe, communal, utilitarian, work-shopped parameters, will of course hate this poem. Mainstream consensus and academic coterie would loath the conflation of cunnilingus with state assassination, of a 'girlfriend's amazing waxing' with Osama bin Laden's own 'beard of hair'. However, the virtuoso juxtaposition of private and public experience is often the realm of great metaphor.

The unmistakable Seidel signature, and the word most often present in reviews of his work, is 'shock'. This stands as much for the shocking content as for the unpredictability of his line of thought, for the shock of the new, the beautiful brutalism of his treatment of sex, medicine, science, money, world travel, current affairs, the truth and aggression of his statements, the excesses of food and drink, the addiction of American Dream materialism, his humour and his menace, the speed of his thought processes from one subject to another and the violence of examining all of this together at will. Among the more common mediocrity of contemporary poetry, the individualism and originality of Frederick Seidel is truly shocking.

Simon Pomery

Regi Claire, *The Waiting*. Word Power. ISBN 9780956628381. PBK. £7.99

Regi Claire has said that *The Waiting* is her 'Scottish novel' and as such it fizzles with the expected trappings: doublings, Calvinism, a gothic air of dreams, mysterious figures and the hauntings of the past, and, of course, a Scottish setting – Edinburgh. Having said that, this is not the city of the usual ghosts and castellated history, but an everyday story of ageing, dog walking and the belated attempt to make sense of a blotchy, inert life and the damning dilemmas of unrealised responsibilities. It is not the trappings which characterise the novel, then, but their undoing in a sensitively drawn tale of female friendship in the face of a particularly feminine onslaught against convention.

'The Waiting' is a stationary but suspenseful title to describe and characterise a restless novel which is constantly on the move, between present and past, home and street, age and youth, resentment and regret, interpretation and its undoing. The narrator, Lizzie Fairbairn, is an ageing widow who has a dog-centric world view, not only in relation to Yoyo her terrier, but to the people around her: her cleaner is 'the Great Dane', her neighbour, 'Miss Chinese Crested' and the students populating the Meadows and its environs, 'greyhounds and Afghans'. Through this confident imposing of schema we suppose Lizzie to be secure in her relationship with her surroundings; yet this humorously realised, crotchety but tolerant certainty will shatter by the end of the narrative. Lizzie's personal and moral weakness is exposed by the return of the past and her relationship with Marlene, a friend since childhood up until her untimely death. Marlene is a rebel, and one question the novel ponders is whether she is corrupt or corrupted by her circumstances; her poverty and illegitimacy, and her persecution, for example, being singled out for the ridiculous rendition of the role of Mary Magdalene in the nativity play. With such painfully ironic touches, Claire toys with fate in a Sparkian mode, pre-figuring characters' endings and trapping them in their stories. This notion of inescapable fate is also insinuated by the chronological manner in which the story of the past is told, making it feel set in its destiny. However, in tension with this predestination Claire highlights the vagaries of existence; these are not lives lived to a scheme but fecklessly fallen upon in moments of vacillation. To the credit of the novel, there are no easy answers provided here, as to whether Marlene is mad or bad, or whether Lizzie is justified in her feelings of guilt for not 'saving' her. These are not made weighty philosophical questions but refer to the agonising everyday decisions necessitated by our responsibilities to others, and are all the more poignant for that. Marlene exemplifies the attraction of those lawless individuals who take all the risks of adventure so we, the convention bound, don't have to, and sidekick Lizzie is caught between desire and disgust.

The past returns in the form of Marlene's grand-daughter Rachel who comes to Lizzie for information about her grandmother. Having carefully constructed her own equanimity in the routines of her life, Lizzie resents this exhortation to excavate her personal history. Her own distraction from the psychic disturbances of the unpleasant past and present is sugar; sweets, biscuits, cake and chocolate are an ever-present obsession in the novel. More than an old lady's indulgence, these are the medicines of forgetting, dangerously over-prescribed in relation to the scavenging Yoyo, who is a symbol of the over-consumption of the leftovers of the past and the sugared confection of the present. This lack of balance makes them both sicken, ultimately keeling over in the dissolution of guilt, blame, dependence and unacknowledged responsibility. Resolution here is as useful as Lizzie's doggy nicknames and Claire resists it in her tormenting ending. Again it is the rendering of the inexplicable nature of the ordinary which characterises the strength of her narrative.

Unusually for a novel about memory *The Waiting* does not deal in an obvious trauma and its recovery from Freudian tinged mind deceptions; it does not wear its reparation on its sleeve. Lives and events here, even the specifically masculine act of suicide, are presented without the aid of the spectacular and sensational, or the melodramatic; Claire's writing is measured, poised and sensitively composed. In particular, it is usual for the mundane materiality of life to interrupt those gothic flashes mentioned earlier, a process I am persuaded must be resonant of ageing. And through this, even because of it, *The Waiting* is a deeply sympathetic novel which resists imposing comprehension, opting instead for thoughtful aggravation of an unsatisfied life and the difficulties in digesting an unresolved past.

Carole Jones

Dear Boy. Faber. ISBN 9780571284054. PBK. £9.99
Emily Berry

'This is a poem about a horse that got tired', begins Robert Creeley's 'Please': 'Poor. Old. Tired. Horse'. 'This is not the horse /which they showed /me yesterday', begins Emily Berry's Creeley-resembling 'Preparations for the Journey': 'Take this horse /back to his master.' The horse 'of which we spoke' duly turns up but not the saddle, which is sadly 'no /good at all'. The girths and stirrups aren't up to much either. The situation looks disastrous, but we're off on our journey anyway: 'Does nothing more /detain us? /Have we forgotten /nothing?' What unites Berry and Creeley's poems is less the horse than the journey, and less the journey than the telling of it. *Dear Boy* is full of poems like 'Preparations for the Journey' in which the awful daring of a moment's surrender overcomes the speaker's hesitations, launching us into strange and possibly entirely misguided journeys and narratives.

Berry likes lists and stories, and lists that tell stories, and especially likes to deflect the messiness of human relationships onto tidier, more manageable liaisons with city pavements ('London Love Song'), foreign semi-autonomous regions ('Zanzibar'), and inanimate objects (such as Lorenzo Pig, 'With his footstool soul / and heart of solid newspaper   he is just exactly like a person / Lovely, Italian leather Lorenzo'). Readers may be reminded of Stevie Smith by Berry's fondness for vaguely melancholy proxies or personae and their tales of comic woe, in poems such as 'Shriek' and 'Hermann's Travelling Heart' – Hermann being, in contrast to the host of inanimate objects vivified by their emotional surrogacy, a real live tortoise who is 'like a statue of a tortoise'.

The *faux-naïve* manner honed by Stevie Smith in the 1930s was partly a response to the all-boys-together nature of the MacSpaunday collective, and in Berry's *faux-naïveté* too one might detect a strategy of dissembling or concealment. While the reader is busy responding to the poems as cultivated acts of winsomeness, the poems are quietly lodging their emotional payoffs somewhere in the reader's unconscious.

Berry's means of going about this are suitably roundabout, however. 'I have discovered the meaning of life and it is curatorial', we read in 'Nothing Sets My Heart Aflame', a funny poem that sends up the contemporary vogue for the vintage.

> I am not the only one for whom the word *vintage* has become like a lozenge

My eyes lounge among the relevant pages of the premier auction website
You will have some experience of this
    Perhaps there was something missing in your life and it was a mid-century lampshade, or a fixed-gear bicycle.

It's a middle-class disease ('When the class war happened one side was busy buying salvaged parquet flooring') and the speaker is not ashamed to show her hand ('I don't know what the other side was doing'). The problem is that 'We've nearly run out of eras', and as the poem reaches its crisis the speaker starts to hyperventilate, along with thousands of readers of the *Observer* lifestyle pages:

I don't know what to do – should I make my own clothing and wear a
    necklace of cotton reels
Should I go to Berlin
But I see something of myself in a Perspex brooch
Give me a moment
I'll be okay after I've looked through this collection of postcards of
    modernist churches

Among these comic studies of contemporary malaise, and amid Berry's wonderfully imaginative story-telling style, the poet has planted a few 'vintage' numbers of her own though, and not always successfully. There are several poems about an inappropriate patient-doctor relationship, for example, that feel a bit like impulse buys on a poetry version of Etsy (the 'vintage' alternative to eBay): instead of a mid-century lamp-shade or a fixed-gear bicycle, we have some 1890s Freudian analysis here, some 1950s confessional poetry there:

'Time is nothing,' says the Doctor.
He's unconventional. 'Time is nowhere,
like a dead bird in a cave. Let's take a look inside.'

[…]

The Doctor bites and leaves a mark
like the fossil of a sprung jaw.
He slapped my face with his penis.

These 'vintage' efforts are rare, and are the only obvious misstep in an otherwise extremely fresh-voiced and intelligent collection; their presence only throws into temporary relief the sharpness and poise we find elsewhere in the book. The consequent (but slight) unevenness in tone is forgivable in a first collection, and asks some challenging questions of the poet; it will be interesting to see how Berry answers.

Read alongside recent and upcoming debuts by Sam Riviere and Heather Phillipson, Emily Berry shows signs of a certain generational *esprit de corps*. All three are characterised by a capacity for eccentric and even startling direct statement. 'My innocence is really incredible', writes Berry in 'David'. *Dear Boy* is the impressive fruit of this enviable condition.

Aingeal Clare

The Home Corner. Faber. ISBN 9780571230617. PBK. £12.99
Ruth Thomas

Ruth Thomas's second, Edinburgh-based novel is told from the perspective of nineteen-year old Luisa McKenzie, who has recently taken a job as a classroom assistant in a local primary school. Less a *Bildungsroman* than a snapshot of a particular moment in a young girl's life, the novel is convincing in its depiction of Luisa's anguish at the choices she has made: while most of her former school friends have disappeared off to university, she is left chanting times tables, organising mid-morning snacks for pre-schoolers, and checking on the class goldfish. Luisa also lives at home, and while her parents are kindly and encouraging, she finds the stifling domestic set-up too much to bear. Looking around her bedroom she observes that it is 'full of things I had outgrown': 'on my pine bookshelves was a half-empty bottle of moisturising cream I'd bought when I was sixteen, and the Mr Men tin I'd had since I was nine'. Earlier, when she bumps into an old school friend in the local supermarket and they compare their evening plans, her own rather parochial routine seems to represent a larger existential failing: 'It was Sunday afternoon, and we were going home to eat tea, and tea was going to be what we usually had on Sundays: bread and cheese and crisps and vinegary beetroot and halved boiled eggs and slices of ham. It was not going to be Thai fishcakes and bottles of beer, it was going to be high tea, with cold cuts'.

The tedium of this day-to-day routine is interspersed with Luisa's memories of her recent schooldays, particularly her relationship with one-time boyfriend Ed McRae, an aspiring artist whose t-shirt is emblazoned with the words *Life's a Bitch and Then You Die*, 'as if he had Life worked out: as if he already knew all its ironies'. This is mere posturing, as Luisa is quick to discover: his parents own a vast house in one of the most affluent parts of Edinburgh, complete with Aga, tasteful Christmas decorations and two cars in the driveway. Things start to derail at this point – in terms both of Luisa's relationship with Ed, and, perhaps just as regrettably, the narrative drive of Thomas's novel. The main problem here is that the central event – the formative experience of Luisa's young life – has taken place in the first sixty or so pages. She gestures towards her earlier trauma in rather oblique terms later in the novel, yet this later reticence serves little or no purpose when we already have most of the details to hand.

Luisa is clearly unhappy in her job, and her colleagues are unimpressed with her lack of application: she is consistently late, and her behaviour in the staffroom veers between gaucheness and awkward reserve. She also shares little in common with the other teachers, most of whom are a great deal older. Some of the characterisation here is deft – Thomas offers a neat thumbnail sketch of head teacher Mrs Crieff, whose uncompromising efficiency prompted her to replace her front lawn with fake grass. We follow Luisa's thoughts as she and her mother stand staring at it from the pavement: 'It was a searing, impossible green. A blackbird had settled on it as we watched, bounced its beak against it and flown off again, puzzled. I'd seen that happen a few times since then: Mrs Crieff's conning of the blackbirds'. Elsewhere the children's various curiosities are suitably whimsical and entertaining, yet Luisa's ennui slowly starts to seep into the narrative, and while minor points of school etiquette give us a sense of the petty protocol she has to put up with, they also drain the plot of vitality and drive: 'at St Luke's it was OK to call the mothers Mum. You could call the mothers Mum but you couldn't call the fathers Dad. It was just one of those things'.

The writing here is competent, if occasionally uneven. Phrases like 'You can try, and fail, despite your best intentions' are nothing if not banal, yet there are flashes of real linguistic flair: Thomas has a fine ear for dialogue, and her rendering of Luisa's awkward social exchanges feels suitably authentic, while the regular flashbacks to Luisa's childhood are immediate and striking: 'The toy cows we had in the Portakabin were exactly like the ones I'd used to play with at home when I was little… And when I looked at them, time seemed to fold up, like a telescope.'

One final reservation relates to the presentation of this book: the cover image and blurb seem to be aimed at a niche female readership, so that while the novel deserves (and may well enjoy) a large fan base, it could end up being read only by teenagers and young mothers.

Alexandra Lawrie

Instant-flex 718. Bloodaxe Books. ISBN 9781852249700. PBK. £8.95
Heather Phillipson

Heather Phillipson's debut collection exists in a suspension of the ordinary. These poems are playful, wry and often absurd, but adhere to a worldview informed by a fierce intellect. Phillipson is by turns postmodern flâneur, poet-philosopher and cultural critic, taking to each of these roles with an affability and flair that in heavier hands might turn to smugness. We can trace a number of influences throughout *Instant-flex 718* (influences Phillipson readily acknowledges), from Frank O'Hara to Heidegger to The Smiths. If this sounds daunting, it does a disservice to the her incisive sense of humour – Phillipson charges from high to low registers with the same irreverence and self-awareness, and often we can't help but laugh along. *Instant-flex 718* opens in a tellingly metaphysical attitude, with a frank and funny poem on childbirth and infancy. To begin at the beginning may strike some as facile, but anyone who presumes to know where this book is going will find themselves proven wrong quickly. 'At First, the Only Concern is Milk, More or Less' destabilises what we have come to expect from poetry on motherhood, and instead we are offered a reduction of this not-quite-universal trope that conveys both the awe and the impossibility of discharging the subjective:

> A dense love is under construction. There is more to say
> and less said – least of all Mother, I can't bear to
> outlive you, which is all, really, that matters.
> Sooner or later, it is actual trousers.

Unusually, Phillipson foregoes an economy of language for the sake of maintaining tone. The book is peppered with vocalisation and digression, little utterances that allow the poems almost to speak themselves off the page. This linguistic fidgeting aligns with Phillipson's neat evasion of realism. We may think we recognise the scenery, but we do not know the play, and the poet invents a vernacular for the script that at times borders on Dadaist. Of course this is deliberate: Phillipson's poetics are manifold, and her poems an amalgam of every material the world throws at her.

It is perhaps for this reason that *Instant-flex 718* occupies a space between cultural zones – there is a sense that the poet is being constantly bombarded with information, and these poems are the dreamlike attempt to catalogue and reckon with the baffling vastness of a zeitgeist. Occasionally this manifests as a sort of loneliness (the flâneur always walks alone), as we can see in poems like 'Ablutions' and 'Devoted, Hopelessly':

> I read the Index of First Lines aloud,
> tell myself 'I need to be alone to be more',
> meet Ben, by chance, by the derelict jobcentre.

> He tells me: 'there's a lot of bad love going around.'
> On the concrete, a snail is a comma
> or an apostrophe, depending on context.

This poem, no doubt informed by the New York School tendency towards the occasional ('I do this, I do that'), acts as a remedy for our post-Confessional hangover. Phillipson remains frank, erudite and airy, dropping lines stark as 'The only men it's safe for me to love are dead' with impressive aplomb before she assures us she means 'O'Hara, Stevens, Berryman'. Rather than shying from the anxieties of influence, Phillipson declares them with bathetic humility. For all its straying into the metatextual, *Instant-flex 718* is not out to prove how clever it is. It's the product of an informed mind, certainly, but one recovering from the digital age's endemic information overload. As Phillipson herself puts it, these are poems for which 'Life is too contemporary [...] a nouvelle gymnasium with fountains of waste paper.'

Heather Phillipson's poems excel as the fizzy reportage of a speaker wrestling with a present moment just a little too large for them. This intensity can prove unmanageable in some of her longer poems, and her lean toward the conversational at times stretches the conceit a little far. However, in a more condensed space she deploys her images with flair and dexterity. In 'Rumination on 25mm of Cotton' Phillipson's gift for minute observation is characterised as a series of metaphors that could serve as a microcosm of her whole poetics. Given an object, she allows her imagination freedom to range from the sublime ('it hangs in night's unbound girdle') to the absurd ('It's the hammerless C-string of the world's stupid piano'). Under such scrutiny, a single thread becomes 'immense'. There is a sense of this immensity throughout Phillipson's book – everything from a salted pretzel to a glimpse of a loved one in profile adopts an almost menacing largeness. *Instant-flex 718* might be taken therefore as an attempt to navigate an expanding vista of experience and raise up a corresponding work of art, a trick mirror so huge 'the universe slackens in its shadow'.

Chris Emslie

Definite Articles: Selected Prose 1973–2012. Etruscan Books and Word Power Books. ISBN 9780956628374. PBK. £14.99
Tom Leonard

There is reasonable cause for concern that the statutory duty of local councils to provide 'adequate library facilities to all persons in their area' has been dangerously undermined by the austerity budget. Tom Leonard's *Definite Articles: Selected Prose 1973–2012* is testament, in its ideas and by its existence, to the fact that the cultural cost of any such tendency would be significant.

'The place where a democratic freedom of encounter with Literature has occurred is in the free public libraries', writes Leonard in an introduction to a collection of poetry*, Radical Renfrew,* and indeed it was as a boy visiting Pollok's public library that he developed his own 'relation to the literary world'. The influence of the self-directed nature of those early studies is in evidence throughout this collection: tacitly, in his opinions and choice of subjects, and directly, in his appeals for others to likewise develop independent responses to literature. Leonard is suspicious of literary society and its cliques, of the canon and of those who define it, and in his writings to this end he is frequently persuasive. It is, however, in those essays that address the ways in which language is used, received and manipulated that Leonard advances his most compelling arguments.

'From a Room in Scotland (2)', the second of three sections selected from his online journal, is one such essay and one in which Leonard restates the message that defines a significant part of his output, namely, that 'diction is an index of class'. This, he says, is what 'I have been banging on about for all these years' and this is the cultural prejudice that he argues is used as a means of validating one mode of literature and language while invalidating others. In scanning the books on the shelves of our once-open libraries this process of invalidation is readily confirmed in the enormous discrepancy one finds between the representation of books written in 'standard English' and those written in the kind of language routinely used by the majority of the population. Nonetheless, it remains a precarious task to try and identify society's role in the imposition of this discrepancy. It is precisely this task that Leonard repeatedly sets out to perform.

Though Leonard feels the need to anticipate the charge it would be a careless reader indeed who discerns an allusion to a linguistic *Iron Heel* of conspiracy in these essays. Fortunately, it is one he seems little troubled by:

If what I'm saying seems too much like a simplistic conspiracy theory, then all I'd say is this: it's not possible for a society to have a mode of production based on economic class… without this being a major determining factor, in the specific matter of language, as to what's considered culturally acceptable.

However, what this collection arguably evidences, though Leonard himself might not entirely agree, is that when we scrutinise everyday cultural occurrences we come to the conclusion that no conspiracy is even necessary. What more frequently gives rise to the invalidation of any mode of literature or language other than one endorsed by 'standard English' is not the maliciousness of a literary ruling elite but rather the complacency of those involved in the publication of the written word, in the broadcasting of the spoken word and of the teaching of language and literature to children.

Leonard's disdain for this stifling of linguistic diversity is particularly strong when those being stifled are those whose development should be being nurtured. His praise for an educational handbook that offers 'systematic methods for teaching those who speak low-status languages to garner some pride in the universal validity of their own specific language form' suggests how, perhaps, we might begin to address this problem. This is also true of his appeal that 'teachers in schools were somehow taught, or were required to find out, the application of their particular discipline to the particular locality in which they live'. There are too few voices airing such views.

This uncommonness of voice is never more discernable than in the two-part essay 'A Taboo Too Far' and 'A Letter'. The first piece addresses inconsistencies in the Catholic church's attitude towards 'maintaining purity' and resistance to rape. It goes on to reveal Leonard's own experience as the victim of rape as a twelve-year-old boy. There are details of the attack and of Leonard's fear; there is the perpetrator's appeal to the young boy to remain silent about what has happened and Leonard's terrified agreement; there is his priest's reaction upon being told of the crime in confession (instead of comfort and support Leonard was given 'a bigger penance than I had ever received in my life before'). There is also reference to 'A Letter' that the adult Leonard wrote to the unknown attacker of his childhood 'imputing to him all the responsibility in every detail for what had taken place that day'. It follows 'A Taboo Too Far' in its entirety.

The inclusion of the letter in this collection of essays is an act of rare generosity and solidarity: generosity to the reader, in giving so much; and solidarity, first and foremost, with those whose need is greatest – those who have been victims of similar attacks in the past, those who are currently victims, and those who will be victims in the future. But it is also a statement of solidarity with those who recognise truth and guilt and a damning of those who do not. Fittingly for a piece by Leonard, it resists being interpreted by the usual literary or political modes. It should be read widely.

Beyond those mentioned above there are a number of other essays of note for which there is no space to comment fully here. They range from the required reading of 'On the Mass Bombing of Iraq and Kuwait' (a pamphlet previous published by AK Press) to a audio recording transcript of a non-plussed Leonard that he made in place of written notes when reviewing a Christian Boltanski exhibition. In fact, the essays are so various that it is a shame that dates and places of original publication appear only inconsistently and that the final-page declaration of sources is so vague. The opportunity to address this shortcoming would be but one of many reasons to welcome a second edition.

Robin Jones

Notes on Contributors

Rachael Boast was born in Suffolk in 1975. Her first collection, *Sidereal* (Picador, 2011), won the Forward Prize for Best First Collection, and the Seamus Heaney Centre for Poetry Prize. *Pilgrim's Flower* is published by Picador in October 2013.

Aingeal Clare has written for *The Guardian*, the *London Review of Books*, and the *TLS*. She lives in Aberdeenshire.

Ian Duhig, a former homelessness worker and now a freelance writer, has written six books of poetry, most recently *Pandorama* (Picador 2010). He works extensively with musicians and this September he will be teaching at Maddy Prior's Stone Barn Project.

Chris Emslie is assistant editor at ILK (www.ilkjournal.com). His poems have appeared in the *Indiana Review, Artifice* and elsewhere. By the time you read this he may be in Alabama, pursuing an MFA and trying not to burst into flames.

Carol Farrelly has just been awarded a Robert Louis Stevenson fellowship. She is currently completing her first novel, *This Starling Flock*. In 2010, she received a New Writers award from the Scottish Book Trust. Her stories have been published in journals such as *Stand* and *New Writing Scotland* and broadcast on Radio 4. www.carolmfarrelly.wordpress.com

Diana Hendry has published three books of poems. *The Seed-Box Lantern: New & Selected Poems* (Mariscat) is due out this autumn. Her young adult novel, *The Seeing*, has been shortlisted for a Costa Award and a Scottish Children's Book Award.

Doug Johnstone is the author of five novels, most recently *Gone Again* (Faber & Faber, 2013). He is also a freelance journalist, a songwriter and musician, teaches creative writing and has a PhD in nuclear physics. He lives in Edinburgh.

Carole Jones is lecturer in English at Edinburgh University. Her interests span gender, sexuality and queering representations in Scottish fiction and beyond. She is the author of *Disappearing Men: Gender Disorientation in Scottish Fiction 1979–1999* (Rodopi, 2009).

Robin Jones works as a freelance press officer to publishers. He is the founding editor of *DIN Poetry* the second issue of which will appear this autumn. He lives in Paris.

Russell Jones is the author of two collections of science fiction poems, *The Last Refuge* and *Spaces of Their Own*. He edited *Where Rockets Burn Through: Contemporary Science Fiction Poems from the UK* and is a guest editor for the *Interdisciplinary Science Reviews*.

Thanks are due to Professor James McGonigal of Glasgow University for helping to arrange my interview with Edwin Morgan.

Alexandra Lawrie is a Postdoctoral Teaching Fellow in English Literature at the University of Edinburgh. Her book *The Beginnings of University English: Extramural Study, 1885–1910* (Palgrave Macmillan) is due to be published in January 2014.

Michael Longley's *Collected Poems* were published by Cape in 2006, his most recent collection *A Hundred Doors* in 2011. He has edited Robert Graves's *Selected Poems* which will be published by Faber later in the year. At present he is completing a new collection.

Martin MacInnes is writing a book about insanity, natural history, exploration and vanishings. His fiction, travel and science writing is published in several magazines and journals.

Vicky MacKenzie is completing a PhD on contemporary poetry and science. She has won the McLellan Poetry Award and the Ruth Rendell Short Story Competition and tutors on the St Andrews Creative Writing Summer Programme.

Paul Maddern gained his PhD from Queen's University Belfast and is Teaching Fellow in Creative Writing at the University of Leeds. *The Beachcomber's Report* (Templar: 2010) was shortlisted for the Eithne Strong Award and won the Bermuda Government Literary Prize for Poetry.

Patrick McGuinness's collections of poems are *The Canals of Mars* (Carcanet, 2004), *19th Century Blues* (Smith/Doorstop, 2007) and *Jilted City* (Carcanet, 2010), which was a PBS Recommendation. *The Last Hundred Days* (Seren/Bloomsbury, 2011) won the Writers Guild prize for Fiction and the Wales Book of the Year, and was longlisted for the Man Booker Prize. His next book, *Other People's Countries*, appears from Cape in 2014.

Martin Philip is a lecturer, writer and musician. He has taught literature and creative writing with the Open University for a number of years and teaches part-time at the University of Edinburgh whilst completing his second novel.

Simon Pomery's pamphlet *The Stream* was published in 2010 by tall-lighthouse. His poetry has appeared in publications including the *Times Literary Supplement,* the *White Review, Poetry London, P.N. Review,* and *Tower Poetry.* He read English at the University of Leeds, at Pembroke College, Cambridge, and studied Creative Writing at St Andrews.

John Redmond teaches Creative Writing at the University of Liverpool. He has two poetry collections from Carcanet. His latest critical book is *Poetry and Privacy: Questioning Public Interpretations of Contemporary British and Irish Poetry* (Seren).

Laura Scott's poems have appeared in various magazines including *Poetry Review, Rialto,* and *Magma*. Her pamphlet, 'What I saw', is coming out in September, published by Rialto. She lives in Norwich.

Zoë Strachan's most recent novel, *Ever Fallen in Love*, was shortlisted for the Scottish Book of the Year Award and the Green Carnation Prize. She lives in Glasgow with her partner, the novelist Louise Welsh. They have lived in Berlin.

Yasmin Sulaiman is a freelance writer, and a University of Edinburgh English Literature graduate. She writes about contemporary books and theatre in Scotland and London, and is a previous winner of the Allan Wright Award at the Edinburgh Festival Fringe.

Andrew Taylor teaches in the department of English Literature at the University of Edinburgh. His most recent book, written with Simon Malpas, is *Thomas Pynchon* (2013).

Linda Tym is Co-Director of the Scottish Universities' International Summer School and holds a PhD in English Literature from the University of Edinburgh. Her research focuses on Scottish and Transatlantic literatures and she has forthcoming publications in *The Journal of the Short Story in English* and in *A.L. Kennedy: Contemporary Critical Perspectives* (Continuum, 2014).

David Wheatley is the author of four poetry collections with the Gallery Press, most recently *A Nest on the Waves*, and edited Samuel Beckett's *Selected Poems 1930–1989* for Faber. He lives in Hull.

How to Subscribe to Edinburgh Review

Individual subscriptions (3 issues annually) £20 within the UK; £28 abroad.

Institutional subscriptions (3 issues annually) £35 within the UK; £43 abroad.

You can subscribe online at www.edinburgh-review.com
or send a cheque to

Edinburgh Review
22a Buccleuch Place
Edinburgh EH8 9LN

Most back issues are available at £7.99 cach.

You'll find the new *Edinburgh Review* website at

http://www.edinburgh-review.com

Please join us on Facebook and Twitter.